Jean-Pierre Bouchard
Annick Larivière

Wonderful
PYRENEES

Photographs by Jean-Pierre Bouchard
Translated by Angela Moyon

ÉDITIONS OUEST-FRANCE
13, rue du Breil, Rennes

Top to bottom:

*The Pic du Midi de Bigorre
seen from Payolle (Hautes-Pyrénées).
The Pic du Midi d'Ossau
(Pyrénées-Atlantiques).
Eus (Pyrénées-Orientales).*

Front cover:
*The Pic du Ger and the hairpin bends
leading up to the Col d'Aubisque
(Pyrénées-Atlantiques).*

Back cover:
*The bear: one of the main symbols
of the Pyrenees.*

The north-east face of the Petit Gabizos from the Arrens - Soulor Pass

INTRODUCTION

The Pyrenees link the Atlantic Ocean and the Mediterranean in a succession of peaks and plains, with mile upon mile of silence broken only by occasional areas of human habitation. It is a line separating Spain and France, bringing together vastly-differing worlds and unrolling a carpet of mountain tops over a distance of more than 310 miles from West to East. Any of the gods of Antiquity could have arranged to meet here and argue over ownership of the kingdom. LLixo, God of Water, would have kept watch over Luchon, Ax-les-Thermes, Cambo, Les Eaux-Chaudes, Cauterets, or Amélie-les-Bains. The kingdom would have been the rightful property of Aphrodite, the Goddess of Beauty, thanks to the slender peaks, circling the corries at Gavarnie, Troumouse, Cagateille, Estaubé, the lakes such as Artouste, Oo, or Bouillouses, picturesque valleys and age-old glaciers. Pan, the God of Nature, would have protected the pottoks (wild horses), bears and izards (mountain goats), along with the forests and alpine flowers. He would also have been the confidant of flocks of sheep and their shepherds, a major feature of any Pyrenean landscape. Even Bacchus, the God of Wine, could have laid claim to the kingdom on the grounds that he had given it Jurançon, Armagnac, Madiran, Banyuls etc. As to the mountain peaks themselves (Vignemale, Aneto, Canigou, Pic du Midi de Bigorre, and Pic du Midi d'Ossau to name but a few), they would have been shown the veneration due to any veritable god.

Man left his mark here very early on his history, in the caves at Niaux, Bédeilhac, La Vache, Isturitz or Fontrabiouse. Prehistoric paintings and engravings show that the Pyrenees were inhabited far back in time. After all, it was in Tautavel, in the Pyrénées-Orientales, that the oldest human skull in Europe was discovered. But it is to the region's religious and warfaring history that we owe the impressive range of buildings, from the stan-

A mosaic of Pyrenean images : a Spanish shepherd, a house in the Basque Country, the Col du Soulor and the Béarn region.

ding stones such as the dolmen in the Basque village of Buluntza and the menhir known as "la Peyre Droite" in the Pyrénées-Orientales to the Romanesque churches dotted along the mediaeval road to Santiago de Compostela. From a later period come the castles, fortresses, and citadels erected by the Cathars.

The assault on the summits and the struggle between Man and Nature for supremacy remain a recent phenomenon, however. Not so long ago, in the 17th Century in fact, the region was usually seen as an impenetrable world that was the haunt of Evil. When spas were first opened, though, people began to make an attempt at taming nature and removing something of its hostility. It was at this time that people began to turn their gaze to the mountain peaks and undertake the very first climbs.

Over the centuries, the Pyrenees have succeeded in retaining their authenticity in the image they project to

the outside world - an image of unspoiled scenery, traditional houses, and their own type of economy. Their apparent handicap, i.e. the fact that they once formed an insurmountable barrier, has enabled them to preserve their heritage. Here more than anywhere else, traditions and language are defended by people with very strong characters. From the Atlantic to the Mediterranean, all of them are determined to safeguard their environment, and the flora and fauna, now protected thanks to the setting up of a National Park, constitute wealth in the real meaning of the word. The Pyrenees are not short of tourist attractions, as proven by the thousands of people who come here every year, winter and summer alike, to enjoy all that the mountains have to offer. This, then, is a brief oversight of the many-faceted Pyrenees - their physical geography, landscapes, people and timeless quality.

THE GEOGRAPHY OF THE PYRENEES

*The Maladeta Range in Spain
seen from the Port de Vénasque in Haute-Garonne.*

The Pyrenees range was formed almost sixty million years ago as a result of a sudden collision between the European landmass and the Iberian Peninsula during the Tertiary Era. Mountains were created, bristling with jagged limestone or granite peaks such as those in the **Néouville, Balaïtous,** and **Maladetta** ranges. Nowadays, the lie of the land can be described in just a few brief strokes. The high altitudes of the central section slope gently down towards the Atlantic Ocean while, on the Mediterranean side of the range, the mountainsides are more rugged. From West to East, there are a dozen or more valleys, most of them lying perpendicular to the main line of the range. These valleys are the work of glaciers which have been eroding the countryside since the Quaternary, uncovering corries and lakes, forming waterfalls and creating tumbling mountain rivers. The climates, too, are markedly different, with a more humid climate to the West than to the East. As to the central Pyrenees, they are too far from the sea air and temperatures are lower.

Yet if we restricted ourselves to these few details, we would be concealing half the truth for the Pyrenees form a frontier range, separating France and Spain. Stretching over a distance of 320 miles, they cover an area of 21,235 sq. miles, most of it in Spain (only 6,563 sq. miles lie within French territory). The range varies in width from 56 to 93 miles, and the slopes are totally different on the North and South sides as regards structure, climate and vegetation.

The Lac de Gaube in Hautes-Pyrénées.

Although five of France's *départements* (Pyrénées-Atlantiques, Hautes-Pyrénées, Haute-Garonne, Ariège and Pyrénées-Orientales)and the southernmost tip of Aude can boast of being "Pyrenean", the highest peaks are to be found in the Hautes-Pyrénées. The highest of all is **Vignemale** (alt. 10,718 ft.), followed by the **Pic de Marboré** (alt. 10,572 ft.), the **Pic Balaïtous** (alt. 10,224 ft.), and the **Pic Long** (alt. 10,374 ft.).

The mountain runs into the plains of Aquitaine and the South of France by means of a narrow, sheer-sided shelf. The rivers of Pau, Oloron, Nive, Adour, Garonne, Ariège and Aude, not to mention the mountain torrents and streams, all tumble down to the fertile

Superbagnères in Haute-Garonne.

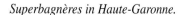

plains in successions of waterfalls. Perched at altitudes of almost 6,500 ft. the villages in the Pyrénées-Orientales are much higher up the mountainside than their counterparts in the Pyrénées Occidentales which huddle at altitudes of between 1,300 and 2,600 ft. Ski resorts have been built at still higher altitudes, among them La Mongie (Hautes-Pyrénées) at 5,850 ft, Les Angles (Pyrénées-Orientales) at 5,200 ft., Les Agudes (Haute-Garonne) and Pyrénées 2000 (Pyrénées-Orientales) at 4,875 ft, Font-Romeu (Pyrénées-Orientales) at 5,037 ft, Gourette (Pyrénées-Atlantiques) at 4,550 ft, Barèges (Hautes-Pyrénées) at 4,063 ft, Cauterets (Hautes-Pyrénées) at 3,250 ft. etc.

In the Spanish provinces of the Basque Country, Navarre, Aragon and Catalonia, the Pyrenees look very different. The range is wider, and it runs down to the Ebre Plain in an orderly fashion. The summits are sharp and jagged for they have escaped the erosion of the Atlantic that has reshaped the other side of the border. In the centre is the Maladetta Range, including the highest mountain in the Pyrenees - the **Pic d'Aneto**. The Spaniards, then, hold the record as regards altitude, with a peak rising to 11,076 ft. It is here, in this well-known area, that the R. Garonne rises.

None of the great Spanish rivers rises in the Pyrenees. The Aragon, Gallego, Cinca, and Segre are

The Arrazas Canyon in Spain.

only minor rivers, flowing into the better-known Ebre and swelling its waters. And in the Spanish *sierra*, the change in climate is obvious in the arid areas gashed by deep gorges, and the difference in vegetation. Near the oak trees and pines are box, almond and olive trees. But the Pyrenees do not only provide Spain with huge stretches of forest that are vital for its economy; they also boast popular ski resorts such as Candanchu, Canfranc, Formigal, Panticosa, Cerler, Super Espot. As to the towns and villages of Pampluna and Jaca, they have a strong sense of Hispanic identity.

On previous pages: The Maladeta Range in Spain, including the highest peak in the Pyrenees - the Pic d'Aneto (alt. 11,076ft.).

The Pont d'Espagne near Cauterets (Hautes-Pyrénées).

The Spanish ski resort of Formigol near the Col du Pourtalet.

THE ETERNAL (EVER-CHANGING) LANDSCAPE OF THE PAST

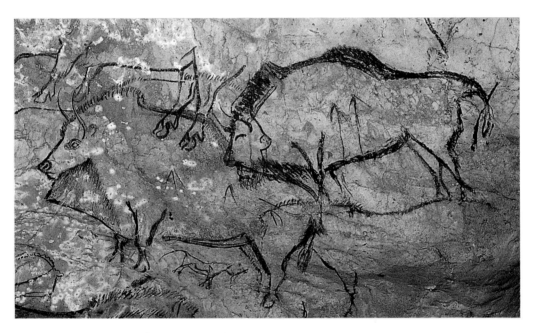

The cave in Niaux in Ariège has one of the finest known examples of prehistoric cave art, with Lascaux and Font-de-Gaume in Périgord, Pech-Merle in Quercy, and Altamira in Spain. Artists working in the Magdalanian Era painted these bison and horses some 14,000 years ago.
Photo by R. Robert.

There is no use seeking any kind of historical unity in the Pyrenees. Although well-defined in administrative and geographical terms, it is more difficult to detect any common past for the people living in an area that stretches from the Roussillon to the Basque Country. There have, of course, been a number of major events and historical periods that have brought people together such as the Battle of Roncesvalles, the life and times of Henri IV, King of France and Navarre, and the Treaty of the Pyrenees, but from Atlantic to Mediterranean the true picture is one of a juxtaposition of tiny territories, each with its own destiny.

The early installation of **prehistoric peoples** is magnificently proven by the paintings and engravings discovered in caves. There are hundreds of caves across the range as a whole, some, but not all, dating from pre-historic times, and twenty-two of them are now open to the public. The high density can be explained briefly in geological terms. The caves were created by the passage of water and the subsequent erosion of the porous lime-stone rock. The "karst" first came into being several thousand years ago, creating an entire network of fis-sures, crevices and increasingly large tunnels which finally formed caves. Underground rivers still flow through some of them. Natural concretions such as sta-lactites, stalagmites, cave pearls, and eccentrics give some of the caves a beauty of their own, e.g. Fontrabiouse in Capcir, Aguzou, Médous, Le Loup and Les Sarrasins near Lourdes, Lombrives and Bétharram, to name but a few. Others, though, contain outstanding

Bédeilhac Cave (Ariège): head of a prehistoric sling made from a reindeer antler. It has been named "the fawn with the bird".

examples of pictorial art. **Niaux, Bédeilhac, Mas d'Azil** and **Gargas** attracted prehistoric men whose skill in depicting animals remains a never-failing source of ama-zement. Engraved or painted on the cave walls are bison, stags, horses, mountain goats, and reindeer, interspersed with symbols that have retained all their original myste-ry. The many prints of mutilated hands in Gargas are among the other enigmas which have not been solved.

Along the ancient pathways followed by the animals and herdsmen when moving up to alpine summer pas-tures are occasional standing stones - dolmens, menhirs, and rocks with strange shapes, left unprotected against

Opposite:The vast Lombrives Cave in Ussat-les-Bains (Ariège).
The Grotte de la Vache, opposite Niaux in Ariège, contains a very large prehistoric site
which has provided flints, weapons, tools, and objects engraved and carved out of bone or reindeer antlers.
Some of the engraved items are masterpieces of Magdalanian graphic art.

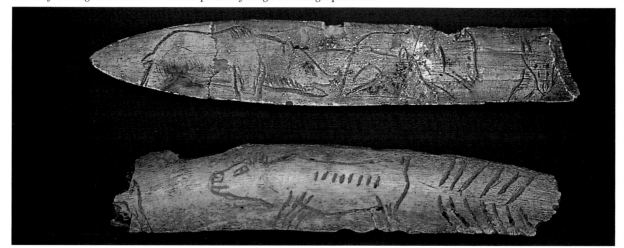

The underground basins in the superb Bétharram Cave which sits astride the departmental boundaries of the Pyrénées-Atlantiques and the Hautes-Pyrénées.

the wind. These mysterious stones, which date from the **protohistoric period**, can be seen right across the Pyrenees. The ones in the Fenouillèdes area, such as the "Peyre Drete", jut up from amidst the juniper bushes, heather, thyme, rosemary and other balmy plants that grow on the scrubby moorland.

Judging from the buildings they left behind, the **Romans** had little effect on the Pyrenees. Today, Roman remains consist of nothing but a few stretches of road, a few bridges, and a few walls, now forgotten. In the Pyrénées-Orientales, the *Via Domitia* was the main route linking Italy to Spain along the Mediterranean coast and it can still be seen running along the mountainside. L'Ecluse has the remains of fortifications from this same period. Yet there are two major features of everyday life that date from the days of the Ancient Romans - spas and wine-growing. Recognised very early on by the Romans for their medicinal virtues, the hot mineral springs of the Pyrenees continued to be used right down to the Middle Ages. Lepers, for example, were treated in

Ax-les-Thermes; later the Albret family and other V.I.P's took advantage of the "waters". And wine was equally popular with the Romans. It is they we have to thank for all the vineyards which now run picturesquely down the hillsides at Banyuls and Collioure.

The onset of the barbarian invasions and the fall of the Roman Empire in the 4th Century, however, marked the arrival of the Dark Ages, a period filled with dire events and disasters.

In the 5th Century, on the West side of the Pyrenees, the Vascones, the ancestors of the Basque people, ruled one-half of the mountain range; to the East were the Visigoths who occupied Septimania. The remainder of the range was annexed to Aquitaine where the Franks held power. After becoming King of the Franks in 768 A.D., Charlemagne methodically undertook to conquer the entire country. At this end of the kingdom of Gaul, security was threatened by the Saracen in Spain. The army set out on a campaign but it was a failure. In 778 A.D, Charlemagne's army, under the command of **Roland**, was

The vineyards in Banyuls on the Mediterranean coast (Pyrénées-Orientales).

Roncesvalles (Spain) : the monument in memory
of Charlemagne's nephew, Roland, who was killed
in 778 A.D. by the Vascones in the Roncesvalles Pass.

defeated at **Roncesvalles** by the Vascones. At that same time, Charlemagne annexed Septimania to the kingdom of Aquitaine. When he died, though, the entire Carolingian empire collapsed and several political enemies came to the fore, among them the Viscounty of Béarn, the Bayonne area, Navarre, and the Kingdom of Catalonia.

It was also during this period that pilgrims began to set out along the highways and byways, on the way to **Santiago de Compostela** in Spain where, it was said, the tomb of the Apostle, St. James the Elder, had been miraculously discovered. The place was to become one of the largest centres of pilgrimage in the Western world. "*El camino frances*" (literally "the French road"), which ran as far as Galicia, crossed the Pyrenees and, in many places along the way, hospitals, churches and abbeys were built to provide care and hsopitality for the pilgrims. Indeed, the pilgrimage route is dotted with Romanesque churches. Morlaas, Lescar, Oloron, Sarrance, Roncevaux and Somport were unhoped-for stopovers.

Romanesque capitals in the churches of Saint-Michel-de-Cuxa in the Pyrénées-Orientales (left)
and Saint-Engrâce in the Pyrénées-Atlantiques (right).

Opposite: Countless Cathar fortresses were built on spurs of rock in the Pyrenees.
Shown here are Montségur in Ariège (top left and bottom right), Peyrepertuse in Aude (top right) and Quéribus (bottom left).
In the centre is a disk-shaped gravestone dating from the days of the Cathars.

The first millenium was followed by a period of renewed interest in building, marked by the beginnings of **Romanesque architecture**. Saint-Martin-du-Canigou, Saint-Michel-de-Cuxa, Saint-Bertrand-de-Comminges, Saint-Engrâce, and Saint-Jean-des-Verges are all outstanding examples of this style, based on care-fully-balanced proportions, the uniform use of volume and the inclusion of semi-rounded barrel vaulting.

In the 13th Century, a power structure based in Catalonia and Aragon seemed to be gaining ground but, in 1213, the final project aimed at establishing a Grand Federation of Pyrenean States crumbled away to nothing with the death of Peter of Aragon at the Battle of Muret.

The **Cathar epic** dates back to this same period. During the second half of the 12th Century, a new religion developed, spreading throughout Southern France. Catharism, which declared itself to be based on Christ and the Gospels, included a Manicheistic view of the universe. It was a protest movement and it enjoyed ever-increasing support. As a result, the Roman Catholic Church turned the full might and power of its wrath against it. Faced with the threat posed by the "heretics", an unusually violent holy war was waged from 1209 to 1229. The crusade against the "Albigensians" ended in the flames that burned many supporters at the stake and in the capture of all the Cathar fortresses. Puivert fell in

1210, Peyrepertuse in 1240, Montségur in 1244 and Quéribus in 1255.

During the century spanned by another, equally famous conflict (the One Hundred Years' War, 1337-1453), another major event took place - and it was of vital importance for Béarn. **Gaston III Phoebus** took advantage of the Franco-English conflict to turn his viscounty of Béarn into a sovereign principality. In the 16th Century, the d'Albret family also carried the kingdom's colours high. Henri IV did not think of annexing the principality to the French crown; it was Louis XIII who decided to do so, in 1620.

In the 17th Century, there was no precise frontier running along the Pyrenees. Citadels and fortresses were still considered to be useful in case of attacks launched by other powers seeking to extend their sphere of influence. Fortifications were built in Bayonne and Saint-Jean-Pied-de-Port. In 1659, the **Treaty of the Pyrenees** finally laid down the precise border between France and Spain, and Louis XIV married the Infanta of Spain, Maria Teresa.

Literary works published in the 18th Century did little to encourage people to see the Pyrenees for themselves. On the contrary, the region was described as "a hostile place, a ravine worthy of the kingdom of Satan". Nobody dared to venture into the mountains; they were the haunt of redoubtable brigands and struck fear into the hearts of many. The difficulties of access, high altitudes, absence of vegetation and sparse population prevented outsiders from discovering the area and its people.

With the development of means of communication and the encouragements proffered by the medical world to breathe pure air and "take the waters", mentalities gradually began to change. In the 18th Century, it became fashionable to **take the waters** and this brought huge numbers of visitors to various spots right across the Pyrenean chain. Within one hundred years, several well-known people had already described the benefits of the mineral spring water. Rabelais and Margaret of Angoulême (King François I's sister) had visited Cauterets, Jeanne d'Albret and Montaigne had gone to Bagnères-de-Bigorre, King Henri IV had stayed in Les Eaux-Bonnes and Les Eaux-Chaudes, and Madame de Maintenon had visited Barèges.

The Pyrenees, with their wealth of hot mineral springs, enjoyed a rapid period of development in the mid 19th Century, during the Second Empire. In addition to Luchon, the most popular of all spa towns today,

The pump rooms in Luchon (Haute-Garonne).

Fun in the mountains: Font-Romeu in the Pyrénées-Orientales (top left) and Roland's Breach in the Hautes-Pyrénées (top right).

In the Campan Valley (Hautes-Pyrénées).

a whole string of other resorts are dotted across the mountains, from the Atlantic Coast to the Mediterranean. Each of them is famous for its ability to cure certain ills and each of the springs is different. In Luchon, Ax-les-Thermes, and Vernet the spring provides hot water that is high in sulphates and sodium. In Bagnères-de-Bigorre, Aulus, Ussat and Capvern, the water is high in sulphate and calcium. In Salies-de-Béarn, it is high in chloride and sodium, and in Le Boulu it is high in bicarbonate of soda.

Another, adventure-packed, attraction followed hard on the heels of the first wave of enthusiasm for the

A pilgrimage to Lourdes in the Hautes-Pyrénées.

Pyrenees - **mountaineering**. How many so-called madmen scaled the invincible peaks? Whether it is historical fact or mere legend, documents dating back to 1276 mention Peter II of Aragon's climb up to the top of the Canigou, from where he could survey his kingdom. In 1787, Louis François Raymond de Carbonnières set off to climb the Pic du Midi. He repeated his exploit thirty-five

Scenery near La Mongie in Hautes-Pyrénées.

times, studying the structure and geography of the mountain as he did so. In 1802, he conquered Mont Perdu. People who came to take the waters and other, less well-informed visitors were to follow in the footsteps of these pioneers. At that time, the clothing worn for mountain-climbing was nothing short of amazing. The outfit worn by the Duchess d'Abrantès in 1809 when she set off to climb Vignemale is worth a particular mention, "Gaiters, nankeen trousers, a cashmir frock-coat, a generous cape, heavy shoes with studded soles and crampons, and a walking stick tipped with izard horn".

In 1858, another type of fervour was instilled into local people. In **Lourdes**, the appearance of the Virgin Mary to Bernadette Soubirous marked the beginning of pilgrimages undertaken by people from all over the world. Nowadays, there are estimated to be more than five million pilgrims in Lourdes every year.

In the 20th Century, the discovery of oil in Lacq set the Pyrenees on the trail of industrial development while tourism, based on the outstanding natural beauty of the mountain range, became a vital source of economic wealth.

WILD LIFE AND PLANTS

An incomparable natural setting:
the corrie at Troumouse in the Hautes-Pyrénées.

Despite having binoculars and camera permanently to hand, today's ramblers have very little chance of spotting any **bears**. How many are there left in the Pyrenees? Probably a dozen, compared to two hundred at the turn of the century. Discredited by the shepherds and the owners of the herds or flocks which they sometimes attacked, bears have been difficult to maintain in their natural environment. Financial compensation has not been sufficient to calm tempers. Since 1972, the bears have been protected by an order totally prohibiting anybody from killing them. Yet the bear remains little more than one element in the folk memory of the Pyrenees. It can be seen on old post cards, beside bear tamers or proud huntsmen, and everything serves as a reminder of the days of major hunts. Hunting trophies on the walls and bearskin rugs beside the bed made the animals part and parcel of everyday life. Even in the kitchen, bear meat was used as the main ingredient in a number of very tasty recipes.

Most of the bears are to be found in Béarn and they are a common topic of conversation. Yet they make mockery of the controversy that they arouse wherever they pass. Between the Aspe and Ossau Valleys, you may, if you are very lucky, find paw prints, tufts of fur

In olden days, bear tamers would travel through towns and villages.

Opposite: A Pyrenean bear. How much longer can this population, which has been part of the local landscape for so many centuries, continue to survive in the Pyrenees?

The izard, or wild goat, has become one of the symbols of the Pyrenees, thanks to its gracefulness and agility. Photo by D. Lardat.

and scratch marks on trees. But bears are mistrustful animals and are only to be spotted for a few, brief moments. In fact, they remain almost totally invisible, hiding in the woodlands of Béarn, on the slopes of the mountains in the Luchon area, in the narrow valleys of the Couseran, in the Aure Valley, or on the Vicdessos and Donezan plateaus. An adult bear can weigh up to 47 stone and stands 6 ft. 6 ins. high on its hind legs. They are powerful plantigrades, only coming out at night in search of fruits such as blueberries, raspberries and blackberries. On the odd occasion when the bears are unable to find any of the mountain food that they are so fond of and begin to go hungry, they may attack ewes and cows.

The **izard** is a graceful, agile animal, light on its feet and very swift-moving, and it is another well-known member of the Pyrenees' animal world. It is a cousin of

A Merens horse in Ariège.

A pottok in the Basque Country, in the foothills of the Rhune.

the Alpine chamois and has a unmistakable outline - slender legs, a strong body, and a high, haughty head crowned with an elegant pair of horns. Its excellent sense of smell and infallible hearing warn it of any approaching danger. Clambering across the walls of rocks amidst the forests on both the French and Spanish sides of the border, the russet, beige or brown-coated izard is threatened by many a predator. One of its best-known enemies is Man, but it is also attacked by eagles, foxes and, more occasionally, bears. Izard hunting has long been a tradition in the Pyrenees and it continues to exist today. However, the setting up of nature reserves, wild life parks and areas covered by protection orders now ensure the safety of the goats.

They are a symbol and many a peak, pass, or difficult gulley bears their name e.g. Col des Isards (Gavarnie), Pic Isaré, Brèche des Isards (Balaïtous),

A delight to the eye during springtime,
to anybody experienced enough to recognise the owner
of this perfect wheel - the rare but majestic capercaillie.
Photo C. Bonnaud.

Piste des Isards etc. Depicted on medallions, the mountain rangers chose the izard as their official badge. And at present, it is a red izard head against a white background that can be seen on the signs indicating the Pyrenees National Park.

How is it that, in Tyrol or Switzerland
Where I went by chance,
There is not a single chamois
That seems to me as beautiful as an izard?
                                    Edmond Rostand, Luchon, 1887

In the Niaux Cave in Ariège and Isturitz Cave in the Basque Country, there are a number of cave paintings and engravings dating from the Magdalanian, representing heads or bodies of horses. These drawings date back thousands of years and serve as reminders of life in those far-off days; they are also strangely reminiscent of the **pottoks** and **Merens horses** we see today. Do the drawings show the ancestors of the horses which now roam at will across the Pyrenean pastures? Research has suggested that this is a possibility.

Pottoks can be seen in Labourd and Lower Navarre. It is a breed of small primitive horse, in fact its name means "small horse" in Basque and it is tempting to refer to it as a pony. An official standard describes the breed as follows: a rustic horse with bay, bay-brown, dark bay-brown/almost black or chestnut coat. Mares stand between 11 and 12 1/2 hands high; stallions between 11 1/2 and 13 hands.

Pottocks used to live in the wild, in the mountains. Then Man tamed them, and trained them for riding, jumping or hacking. There is a Pottock Festival every summer. Carriage-driving competitions and show jumping are colourful events.

From May to October, Merens horses live like their ancestors on the pastures in Ariège. With no hersdman and no geographical restrictions other than the peaks along the border with Andorra, the horses can graze on the lush, green grass and take full advantage of their freedom. The Merens horse is gentle, strong and elegant but also has a great deal of endurance. In short, it has many good qualities and whether it is a small horse or a large pony it can be used for every conceivable type of leisure activity. It is a mountain breed, well-known for its skill, good health, robust constitution, and love of hard work. Stallions stand over 14 hands high; mares very slightly less. Its pure black coat with slightly flecked sides is much appreciated. The Merens was used, for many years, as a farm horse but is now ridden and is particularly suitable for hacking and carriage-driving.

In addition to the bears, izards, and horses, the Pyrenees boast many other animals, among them the capercaillie or wood grouse, the male having a black plumage that distinguishes it easily from the russet-coloured female. The ptarmigan is a skilled mimic that blends easily into the environment. White in winter and beige, grey or black thereafter, it can only be seen by birdwatchers with good eyesight. The Pyrenees is the only place in France where you can see the **largest birds of prey** living in the wild. They include lammergeiers which have a wing span of almost 10 ft, fawn vultures, Egyptian vultures also known as Pharaoh's chickens, ravens (wing span 3 ft. 3 ins), kites, falcons and many more. Storks, cranes, passeriforms and ring-doves also fly swiftly over the mountain tops, following their migratory routes.

The Pyrenees has an outstanding natural environment and the flora is as rich and varied as the fauna. Remarkable specimens of edelweiss, rhododendron, narcissi, Ramondia, Pyrenean lilies, and Lapeyrousse pansies are a delight for botanists and walkers alike. There are a thousand varieties of plants, almost one-third of the entire plant heritage of France as a whole. Flowers, moorlands and forests cover the mountainsides while rushing streams tumble down to the valley floors. Up the slopes grow oaks, beeches and pines, birches and rowans. Then, at higher altitudes, the pine forests give way to sporadic stretches of moorland. Towards the summit, rocks and scree alternate with snow, ice, mosses and lichens.

The aconitum napellus or common monkshood.

THE PYRENEES NATIONAL PARK

Set up in 1967, the Pyrenees National Park is one of the oldest in France and it provides an area of 176 sq. miles of unspoilt environment, just waiting to be discovered. Backing onto Spain over a distance of more than sixty miles, it includes picturesque Pyrenean villages and stretches from the Upper Aure Valley in the East to the Upper Aspe Valley in the West. The aims of a national park, which may at first sight appear to be somewhat contradictory, are to conserve the natural heritage and develop scientific research by observation of wild life, while encouraging visitors to come and see for themselves the beauty of the landscapes. However, strict regulations limit the activities of walkers and hikers and failure to comply with them may result in severe punishment (fines and prison sentences). The best solution is to do no more than look, taking time to study the bowl-shaped valleys, the gigantic marks of the glaciers of the Quaternary Era, the lakes, peaks, vast alpine pastures, and a whole range of rare plants. Occasionally, you may be lucky enough to spot izards, ermines, marmottes, hares, capercaillies, ptarmigan, or the *desman* and *euprocte* that are found only in the Pyrenees. The Park Authority manages a natural nesting ground for fawn vultures that extends over 82 hectares. It was set up in 1974. Thanks to scientific monitoring, vultures are able to reproduce in the best possible conditions.

The National Park invites visitors to walk, look, observe, and admire nature - and meet the people who work there, first and foremost the shepherds, herdsmen and producers of ewe's milk cheese.

THE PYRÉNÉES-ATLANTIQUES

The Rhune seen from Hendaye.
the Pyrenean peaks on the Atlantic coast.

THE BASQUE COUNTRY

The *département* of **Pyrénées-Atlantiques** consists of two very distinct entities - Béarn and the Basque Country. Each area has its own natural environment, people and customs.

The Basque Country stretches from mountainside to ocean shore in a never-ending succession of changes. Most of the population lives along the coast and, from Biarritz to Hendaye, there is a whole string of picturesque harbours while the more rural hinterland looks towards the high summit of **Pic d'Orhy** (alt. 6,555 ft). The Basque Country is not only divided between ocean and mountain; it is equally divided between Spain and France. On the French side of the border, it includes three provinces i.e. **Labourd**, the coastal strip round Bayonne, **Lower Navarre**, the area of hills and lower mountains around Saint-Jean-Pied-de-Port, and **Soule**, the more mountainous region with its main town, Mauléon.

On the other side of the border, it is still "Euzkadi", but with four provinces - Navarre, Alava, Biscaye and Guipuzcoa. The Spanish Basque Country constitutes a vital economic and political force. Indeed, along with Catalonia, it is one of the most highly-industrialised regions in Spain.

The origins of the Basque people remains an unsolved mystery, despite much research. Various hypotheses based on migrations of peoples from Africa and Asia failed to convince anybody. Nowadays, specialists tend to support the theory that the people settled here thousands of years ago. The results of archaeological digs prove the existence of a human presence here at least 15,000 years ago.

As to the Basque language, "*euskara*", it remains another mystery that is equally difficult to solve. Its roots seem to go back to the most distant periods of Prehistory. It is often compared to the Hamitic languages of Iberia or the Caucasus, but it has survived every invasion and resisted every attempt at domination. It is still spoken every day, and is hotly defended.

The region's destiny has been very different on each side of the Pyrenees. It is equally different in the three French provinces of Soule, Labourd and Lower Navarre.

History, then, left its mark on the Basque Country very early on. The prehistoric caves in **Sare, Itsuritz** and **Oxocelhaya** bear witness to the existence of a

On previous pages: Scenery in the mountains of the Basque Country.

A Basque house.

population in the earliest days of human development. The numerous dolmens and cromlechs scattered throughout the countryside serve as reminders of an ancient pastoral civilisation. Since these protohistoric times, there has always been a tradition of transhumance. Dolmens can be seen in Bulunzta, Xubera Xain Harria near Saint-Jean-Pied-de-Port and Les Aldudes. The Iparla menhir is to be found in Bidarray. There is also a menhir in Artzamendi and a number of cromlechs. In Béarn, places of particular interest include Bescat, Escout, and Les Aldudes. The Romans were interested in the iron, copper, silver and lead mines in Navarre and the Biscaye area. This peaceful era came to an end with invasions by Germans. They were followed by Vandals, Goths, Vascons and, later, Vikings, all of whom sowed civil disorder. One of the major events in history was the ambush set for Charlemagne's nephew, Roland, near Saint-Jean-Pied-de-Port. Another, in 778 A.D., was the crushing defeat of Charlemagne's rear guard by the Vascones at the Roncesvalles Pass. In the 12th Century, the Labourd area became an integral part of the Duchy of Gascony and fell into English hands when Duchess Eleanor of Aquitaine married Henry III Plantagenet.

The French victory at the end of the One Hundred Years' War, however, brought it back to the crown of France in 1451, where it was to remain. A further feature of the Labourd area was that it had a coastline from which whale fishermen and intrepid navigators set off for adventure on the high seas. In the 18th Century, many of those born in the Basque Country or Béarn set sail for the West Indies - and large numbers of them settled there. Trade brought wealth to the hinterland and enabled local people to discover "exotic" foodstuffs from the tropics such as cocoa, coffee, and sugar cane. In many ways, the Soule area had a similar experience but its annexation to Béarn in 1449 took it into different spheres of political influence, which were quashed by Louis XIII in 1620. As to Lower Navarre, its history is one with that of Béarn, both regions being controlled by great noblemen. One of the most brilliant characters in local history, apart from Gaston Phébus and Henri IV, was Sanche the Great. His vast kingdom stretched beyond the Pyrenees into Castile, Aragon and Leon, making him the most powerful Basque monarch in Navarre. On 4th March 1790, the National Assembly brought the three Basque

Merino sheep.

provinces and Béarn together into one unit with a single destiny when they created the *département* of Basses-Pyrénées.

In the Basque Country, it is no exaggeration to say that History made Man. The locals are determined, independent, proud of their origins, fond of their traditions and only too ready to proclaim their cultural identity. The language, dances, festivals, games and sports reveal the true Basque character in all its originality and authenticity.

The games have been handed down through the centuries and are now part and parcel of daily life. Each village has its own *pelote* court, and it is as important to the villagers as the church or the school. Indeed, courts can be found wherever there are Basques - in Paris, Argentina or even Mexico. Based on the real tennis that was fashionable in the 17th Century, **pelote basque** is a complex game that demands speed, a good eye and very quick reactions. There are several types of *pelote*, the most popular being played bare-handed. They are called *pala corte, petit chistera, joko garbi, rebot, grand chistera, cesta punta, place libre, main-nue, trinquet la paleta, pala ancha, paleta cuir, pasaka* etc. Here, *pelote* is a national sport, just like rugby. It gives an opportunity for major tournaments and festivities which the Basques would not miss for anything in the world.

People here certainly know how to enjoy themselves and festivals are an oft-repeated opportunity to wear the traditional white and red clothes and matching beret which, for many, is their everyday headgear. There is the Cuttle-fish Festival in Hendaye, the Tuna Festival in Saint-Jean-de-Luz, the Ham Festival in Bayonne etc. Local food, which is highly thought of throughout the area, fully deserves its reputation. Near the coast, it is fish that has pride of place - cod *à la biscayenne* or cod *pil-pil*, stuffed cuttle-fish, hake *à la koskera*, grilled bream, sardines, elvers etc. All over the Basque Country, you can enjoy the characteristic *piperade*, Bayonne ham, foie gras, duck fillets, stewed rabbit or game, Espelette pimentoes, *achoa* (a mince dish made from shoulder of mutton), *pantxeta* (the local haggis), *tripotxa* (a sort of tripe sausage) and much, much more. Garlic, onion, tomato and sweet pimento are used to make the tasty Basque sauce which is such a wonderful accompaniment to chicken and other meat. As to the desserts, what words are there to describe the inevitable *gâteau basque* with its creamed almond filling or the *partiza* oozing with black cherry jam? The cheeses, too, hold their own whether they are made with ewe's or cow's milk. The only wine in the Basque Country, *Irouléguy*, is a red or rosé *appellation contrôlée*. The methods used to produce the wine have

On the hairpin bends in the mountains of the Basque Country.

been handed down through successive generations (since the 11th Century), as they have for Izarra liqueur. Some twenty Pyrenean and oriental plants are required to produce the liqueur, which has been manufactured since 1903 in huge copper stills.

From the coastline of the Basque Country, where once local fishermen set off to catch whales and which are now the haunt of surfers, the road runs inland through the Labourd area. The major harbour town, **Bayonne**, lies on the Bay of Biscay; it grew up around the confluence of the rivers Adour and Nive. Its forerunner, in the 3rd Century, was the Roman hillfort of Lapardum, part of which can still be seen today. In the Middle Ages, the flags flying in Bayonne sometimes bore the English leopard and sometimes the French fleur-de-lys. When it became an English town, after the marriage of Duchess Eleanor of Aquitaine and Henry III Plantagenet, it began to enjoy a period of marked prosperity, thanks to flourishing trade. It was in the 13th Century that work began on the building of **St. Mary's Cathedral** whose 276-foot spires are a reflection of its overall size. Just beside it are Gothic cloisters containing a number of tombs and funeral niches.

At the end of the One Hundred Years' War, in 1453, Bayonne again became French. In order to ensure that the town was well defended, Charles VII decided to order the building of the austere **Château Neuf** (New Castle), with its enormous towers and its 10-foot thick walls, on the hill at Mocoron. In the 17th Century, the town walls and citadel designed by Vauban made this the "Key to the South-West" and, with the development of trade, the town enjoyed a golden age of prosperity in the 18th Century. The West Indian trade route was established and trade with the colonies was at a height. The architecture reflected this expansion, giving Bayonne the appearance it still has today in the old urban districts. At present, the harbour ranks among the ten most dynamic and forward-looking ports in France.

In the Saint-Esprit, or Holy Spirit, District, the most interesting buildings are the Gothic church of the same name and the citadel built to designs by Vauban, a typical piece of 17th-century military architecture. Petit Bayonne ("Little Bayonne") is a colourful district with red and green-shuttered houses lining a wonderful labyrinth of arcaded streets and lines of arches. There are two museums here - the **Basque Museum** in a superb Renaissance house, containing an exhibition of the arts, crafts and traditions of the seven Basque provinces, and the **Bonnat Museum** with its superb art collection including sculptures, drawings, and paintings by the

Bayonne and St. Mary's Cathedral.

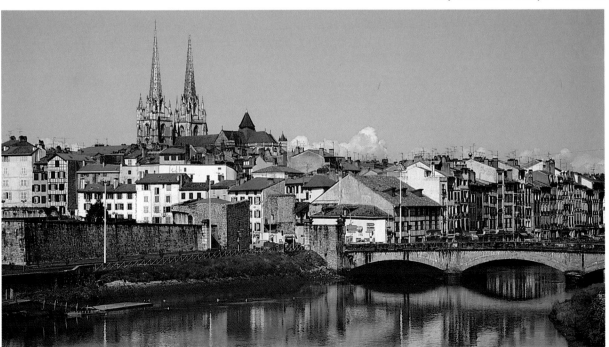

greatest of the Old Masters (Rembrandt, Michaelangelo, Rubens etc.). The Château Neuf stands like a lookout post, but it has nothing to guard any more and the nearby town walls have lost their effectiveness. Turn back to the main part of Bayonne in the shadow of St. Mary's Cathedral. The Rue du Port-Neuf and Rue d'Espagne are bustling shopping centres lined with arched houses decorated wth superb wrought ironwork and half-timbered walls. A few stretches of Roman wall have been integrated into some of the old houses. Another stroll brings us to the mediaeval fortress, the Château Vieux (Old Castle), and the vast town hall housed in the former theatre designed by Charles Garnier, past 18th-century townhouses, and squares, and on down to the quaysides flanking the Nive and Adour rivers.

In Bayonne, which has been famous since the 16th Century for its chocolate-makers, festivities are "explosive" events, whether they take place in the arenas or in the streets, when cattle races set the pulses of the locals beating.

The long sandy belt that forms the seashore in the Landes gives way to a rocky coastline in the Basque Country. The shore bristles with jagged cliffs breaking into headlands, creeks, and isolated rocks, beaten by the crashing ocean. Along with the rocks and the sunshine, water is a vital part of life in **Biarritz**, the world-famous seaside resort. Little is known about its origins. In the 12th Century, the English monarchs who were the masters of Aquitaine took possession of a modest village that was home to fishermen and peasants. In the centre of the oldest district stands the Gothic Church of St. Martin, the oldest building in Biarritz. The harbour is the town's second area of development. Its age-old tradition of seafaring serves as a reminder of the days when whalers could be seen in the Bay of Biscay, from the 7th Century onwards. The capture of the huge marine mammals brought business to all the harbours along the coast. In the Middle Ages, the whales showed a preference for the temperate waters of the Atlantic but, by the 16th Century, they were beginning to become a rare

Opposite: Bayonne.

The Virgin Mary Rock in Biarritz.

*Biarritz: the Belza Villa (or Dark Villa) (top left),
the main beach (top right), and the Orthodox Church
built in 1892 by the Russian colony.*

sight. High above the "Old Harbour" in Biarritz is the
Atalaye Plateau, once an observation platform used by
whale-spotters. Nowadays, it is the site of the Maritime
Museum. When whales began to become scarce,
Biarritz fell into a decline which lasted from the 17th to
the 18th Centuries. Seafarers turned instead to trade
with the colonies, and set off on a different type of
adventure. In the 18th Century, the new "Fishing
Harbour" was built and its predecessor was abandoned,
having been judged too dangerous. On St. Martin's
Headland, there is a lighthouse with 256 steps. From the
top, there is a breathtaking view of the coastline from
the Basque Country up to the Landes.

Biarritz' revival was launched with the fashion for
seabathing. In the 19th Century, Empress Eugénie and
Emperor Napoleon III left their mark on the town. The
Emperor ordered the building of a sumptuous villa, now
the prestigious luxury Hôtel du Palais. Biarritz confir-

Biarritz: the fishing harbour in the shadow of St. Eugénie's Church, and the former Hôtel d'Angleterre.

med its purpose as a cosmopolitan, aristocratic seaside resort and, as the decades passed, the town acquired luxury hotels, coastal villas (Belza, Fal, Javalquinto etc.), churches of various religions, and casinos. Nowadays Biarritz, the famous resort known as the European capital of surf-boarding that plays host to several film festivals, has, without doubt, a great deal to offer. Its beaches (Miramar, Grande Plage, Plage des Basques), cliffs, and hydrangea-lined footpaths make it particularly attractive. As to the Virgin Mary Rock, one of the town's most famous sights, it owes to Gustave Eiffel the iron footbridge that links it to *terra firma* and to a pious man by the name of Biarrot the bronze statue lifted into place at the top of the rock in 1864.

The beaches at Biarritz run along the coast to **Anglet**, forming an extension to the resort. Unlike the villas in the *pignada*, the VVF holiday village at the Chambre d'Amour is resolutely modern in style.

The Chapel of St. Mary Magdalen in Bidart.

Bidart is a delightful village, with its Chapel of St. Mary Magdalen standing high above the ocean. Equally charming are the harbours of **Guétary** and **Ciboure**, one of which is famous for its beaches and its square with the *pelote* court, while the other is well-known for its links with the composer, Maurice Ravel. On the jetty that bears his name stands his birthplace, which has something of a Flemish air about it.

A huge fort dating from 1627 still stands guard over the entrance to the harbour of **Socoa**, now the haunt of yachtsmen. A strait separates Ciboure from **Saint-Jean-de-Luz**. Once a whaling port and, later, famous for its privateers, the town boasts some superb buildings. Louis XIV's house, a particularly fine townhouse, was the idyllic residence of the royal couple, while Maria Theresa of Austria stayed nearby in the Infanta's House. The ornate Church of St. John the Baptist was the setting for the marriage of the royal visitors on 9th June 1660. In the harbour today, there are rows of vividly-coloured fishing boats with evocative names such as *Vagabond*. They raise their anchors and set off in search of the sardines, anchovies and cuttle-fish that are so popular in the Basque Country.

The coast road runs on to **Hendaye**, the last seaside resort in the Basque Country. Chingoudy Bay has a large number of fishing harbours and yachting marinas. **Hendaye** is a border town, separated from Spain by the

Hendaye.

The harbour at Saint-Jean-de-Luz.

R. Bidassoa. Across the water lies **Fuentarrabia**, which may be Iberian but is undoubtedly Basque - and for ever!

Just behind the coastal belt are a number of superb houses. Near Urugne stands the **Château d'Urtubie**, a 14th-century manorhouse with a decidedly defensive

The waters of Hendaye harbour combine with those of Fuentarrabia in Spain.

appearance. **Abbadia Castle**, with its crenelated towers, was designed by Viollet-le-Duc. It stands on the hillside above Hendaye.

The interior of the Labourd area is full of places of architectural interest. In **Espelette**, there is a mighty mediaeval castle that has been turned into the town hall. The Witches' Castle in **Saint-Pée-sur-Nivelle** serves as a reminder of the numerous heretics who were accused of witchcraft and burnt at the stake. The **castles** in **Guiche** and **Bidache** were in their turn owned by the cruel Lords of Gramont, and they lived through many a danger. All that remains of Guiche Castle are the ruins of a square tower; Bidache is a fragile shell. **Sare**, best known for its caves and the clearings used in the shooting of ring-doves in Sayberri and Etchalar, is a "must" on any itinerary. The old districts of Lehenbiscay and Ihalar contain rows of 16th-century dwellings, including the superb Ibarrart farmhouse. The Hôtel de la Rhune in **Ascain** once played host to the novelist **Pierre Loti**. He wrote *Ramuntcho* there in 1897. In the distance is the **Rhune** mountain range, including moorland that is a

delightful place for a walk or a ride on the rack-railway. This is the haunt of pottoks (wild horses) and the mysterious "Betisoak" cattle.

The church in **Ainhoa** has a nave with carved wood panelling; the village, little more than one street, is dotted with houses built in the local style in the 18th Century. **Cambo-les-Bains** is a spa town built in terraces overlooking the river Nive and has played host to VIP's such as Montesquieu, Napoleon III and Empress Eugénie. **Edmond Rostand** had a superb villa, called "Arnaga" built there. St. Lawrence' Church has three storeys of ornate timber galleries and is a fine example of the regional style. Before setting off along the **Imperial Mountaintop Road**, stop and take a look at **Hasparren**. Situated near the famous prehistoric caves at Isturitz and Oxocelhaya, it is the centre of a whole network of protohistoric walls and a crossroads on the routes followed by pilgrims in the Middle Ages. Sights include the home of the poet, **Francis Jammes**, and the Church of St. John the Baptist which contains a Roman stele carved with the story of Novempopulana in Latin. **Arcangues**, which will always be associated with the popular singer **Luis Mariano**, attracts countless fans who come to place flowers on his grave. The furnishings in the Church of St. John the Baptist are as remarkable as the graveyard with its tabular disc-shaped gravestones. In the rustic setting around the village of **Itxassou** lies the Church of St. Fructueux, one of the finest churches in the Labourd area. Only a few miles away is **Roland's Leap**, a rock split into two that is steeped in legend. It is said that, when Roland was fleeing from the Vascones, his horse's hooves cut a gash in the rock - or perhaps it was the valiant warrior's sword.

And on into Lower Navarre, to Saint-Jean-Pied-de-Port, a veritable open-air museum. It gets its name (literally, St. John at the foot of the "port") from its geographical situation at the foot of the "port" or mountain pass at Roncesvalles. It lies not five miles from the Spanish border. The town walls, citadel designed by

Opposite: the Rhune (alt. 2,925 ft.).

Saint-Jean-Pied-de-Port (below and overleaf).

Vauban, Bishop's prison, churches of St. Eulalie d'Ugange and Notre-Dame, bridges over the Nive, old cobbled streets, and Navarre, St. James' and France Gates are superb. Not far away is **Saint-Etienne-de-Baigorry**, another town that is well worth a visit. The church, St. Stephen's, contains a listed altar screen. There is also a Roman bridge and the old districts of Banca, Aldudes, and Urepel. What legends surround Hell's Bridge at **Bidarray**! Satan, who was totally incapable of learning to speak the Basque language, threw himself off the bridge, it is said, and drowned himself in despair. **Saint-Palais** is a major point along the road to Santiago de Compostela. The Lower Navarre History Museum has exhibits describing the town, the region and the history of the mediaeval pilgrimage. **La Bastide-Clairence** was a new town, founded in the 14th Century by Louis X the Stubborn and often hosted the assembly of the States of Navarre. It has a central square flanked by arcaded houses with half-timbered walls, and the superb Romanesque doorway on the Church of Our Lady of the Assumption is also worth seeing. Near the delightful village of **Iholdy** lies **Irissary**, the impressive commandery of the Knights of St. John of Jerusalem.

Mauléon, the main town in the Soule area, consists of an Upper and a Lower Town. In the former, there is a fortress which has stood on this spot since the 12th Century. At its foot is the modern town, but even here there are a few old houses with character, among them the Montréal Residence (now the town hall), and the Renaissance Maytie d'Andurain Residence. The origins of **Tardets-Sorholus** date back to an early shrine built on the Mont de la Madeleine. In 1280, the first fortified village was built, overlooking the river Saison. The valley is full of rural houses, slate-roofed and stone-walled, in a style that is typical of the mountain areas of the Basque Country. There are also a number of outstanding Romanesque churches e.g. **Laguinge Restoue, Sunhar, Haux, Gotein-Libarrens, Idaux,** and **Mendy**. Listed as a historic monument, **Saint-Engrâce** provided lodgings and sanctuary for pilgrims on their way to Santiago de Compostela. Magnificent pictorial capitals illustrate,

Top: Notre-Dame Church in Saint-Jean-Pied-de-Port.

Bottom: Ancient disk-shaped gravestones in Saint-Engrâce cemetery.

Overleaf: the Romanesque Church of Saint-Engrâce.

with a naivety that is particularly expressive, scenes from the Bible and from everyday life. Further north, the Romanesque-Byzantine Church in **St. Blaise' Hospital** was also a stopover along the pilgrimage route. With its layout in the shape of a Greek cross and its octagonal dome, the church is unusual for the marked Oriental influence visible in the layout, doors and windows.

Nature, too, has treasures to share - the **Saint-Engrâce Canyon, the Kakoueta Gorge, the Holcarte Crevice, the Iraty Forest** (the largest beech grove in Europe), the **Arbailles Range, the Osquich Pass** - to name but a few.

THE BEARN REGION

Béarn still resounds to the names of the intrepid lords whose bravery and daring have gone down in history. There were few events of any importance during the pre-historic period or the first one thousand years A.D. but, in the 11th Century, the region made its mark with Gaston IV the Crusader. At that time, Béarn was a small principality centred on Oloron and Lescar. By rallying the Montaner area to the East and other territories to the North-West, Prince Gaston IV created a more extensive kingdom, with precisely-defined borders. He set off on

The "Man from Béarn", "Navarre", the "Gay Old Spark", such were the nicknames given to Henri IV who, after countless adventures, finally conquered the throne of France and became the most popular and most truculent sovereign the country ever had. The statue stands at the entrance to Pau Castle.

In Pau Castle: the tortoiseshell that was Henri IV's cradle, and his white plume.

the First Crusade and gave his support to another cause which was to be his downfall - the Reconquest of Spain. Gaston IV's tomb can still be seen in Saragossa.

Throughout Béarn, the main towns were, at that time, bustling market towns, filled with the sights and sounds of everyday mediaeval activities. Morlaas was, for almost four centuries, the seat of the Viscounts of Béarn. In the 13th Century, Gaston VII transferred his capital to Orthez. Foreseeing the dangers inherent to Franco-English influence on every front, he ordered the building of systems of defence. Orthez was given fortifications; Moncade a castle. Town walls were built around Sauveterre, Pau, Morlaas, Oloron, Navarrenx etc. and a fortress was erected in Montaner.

Béarn was ruled by viscounts and was dependent on the Duchy of Gascony. From the 9th Century onwards, the viscounty was ruled by a succession of dynasties (the Centulles, Moncades, and Foix-Béarn), all of whom swore an oath of allegeance to the Kings of France. When the Duchy of Gascony fell into English hands and the One Hundred Years' War broke out in the 14th

Century, the Viscounts of Foix-Béarn found themselves in an uncomfortable position. Should they recognise the English monarchs or support the Kings of France? The solution was provided by Lord Gaston Phébus who had governed the region since 1343. Taking advantage of the troubled times, he declared Béarn to be an independent, sovereign state. **Gaston Phébus** was one of the first lords to leave his mark on local history. He held court in Orthez, leading a life of luxury and opulence, and left a few reminders of his reign in the town's architecture. A huge brick keep was built to back up the castle in Pau and fortifications or systems of defence changed the Béarn-style buildings erected by Gaston VII in earlier times.

In 1484, a new dynasty strode onto the stage - the **Albrets**. Pau, which had been the capital of Béarn since 1460, was to grow in size and beauty. The sovereigns paid particular attention to the castle. In 1555, Jeanne d'Albret was given the title of Queen of Navarre. She had a very strong Protestant faith, and her coming to power seemed to tip the balance of the kingdom's destiny. Jeanne governed with a firm hand and the State,

The castle and river in Pau.

much to the displeasure of the King of France, fully intended to keep its political and religious independence. The Queen placed all her hopes in her son, Henri, and was determined to make him a perfect defender of the Reformed Religion. Destiny, though, took Henri far away from the place of his birth and, in 1589, he was crowned **King Henri IV** of France, after abjuring his mother's religion.

Pau is best-known as the birthplace of a King of France. It is too often forgotten that the town was also the birthplace of a King of Sweden and Norway. On 26th January 1763, **Jean-Baptiste Bernadotte** was born here. After a meteoric rise through the ranks of the army, he was appointed Lieutenant to Napoleon Bonaparte, with whom he did not get on. He was a skilful warmongerer and won fame at the Battle of Austerlitz and Lübeck. But deep differences of opinion drove the two men further and further apart until the King of Sweden, who was seeking an heir, offered Bernadotte the title of Crown Prince. Thus it was that, in 1818, he became King Charles XIV of Sweden and Norway.

It would not be right to close the list of noteworthy people without a mention of those loyal sons of Béarn who were devoted to their king, Louis XIII. They were none other than the very popular **Three Musketeers** who were so well described by Alexandre Dumas.

Warmongerers, great lords, gentlemen, pilgrims, merchants, all of them have left their mark on Béarn, a natural route to Spain via the Somport Pourtalet or La Pierre-Saint-Martin Passes. The historical trails leading through the land of Henri IV and following in the footsteps of the Lords of Béarn provide superb trips from castle to keep, from beauty spot to town. All these places fill a long page in the history of the Pyrenees.

Pau, the royal town and capital of Béarn, is our first stop. Chosen for its natural strategic advantages, the defensive hillfort of Pau was an ideal lookout post, high above the valley. So it was that, c.11th Century, the famous castle was built. It was to become the residence of a whole succession of great noblemen. The Montauser Keep and Mazères Tower are the oldest parts of the castle. **Phébus** added a mighty, brick-built keep

Overleaf: The Boulevard des Pyrénées in Pau and its panoramic view of the mountains, including the Pic du Midi d'Ossau.

The castle district in Pau.

designed in accordance with the usual building techniques used in Languedoc. He completed his system of defence with the Billère and Monnaie (Mint) Towers, and added a drawbridge, the main apartments with a great hall and kitchens decorated with superb fireplaces, and a guardroom. During the Renaissance period, the castle underwent considerable alteration. It was Margaret of Angoulême who commissioned the frontage of mullioned windows and carvings, a wonderful straight staircase leading up to the throne room on the first floor, and the layout of a park. It was in one of the bedrooms that **Henri IV** was born, on 13th December 1533. The tortoiseshell that was his cradle is carefully and proudly preserved. The French Revolution caused little damage in the castle. A few statues were mutilated and parts of it were used as stables and barracks. In the 19th Century, one final tower was built - the Louis-Philippe. And the palace, which is now a national museum and is one of the most popular tourist venues in France, has come down through the ages almost totally unscathed. It alone summarizes the history of Pau; it is both the heart and the folk memory of the town.

Pau, once a royal residence, has retained all the original atmosphere in its old urban districts. Walk downhill into the picturesque Hédas district, stroll on to the Place Reine-Marguerite, place Royale and place Gramont, take a long look at the wonderful Navarre Law Courts and the Gassion Residence, and step inside the Franco-Swedish Museum that was once the home of Jean-Baptiste Bernadotte. Pau also deserves the title of "Queen of Sports". It pioneered aviation with the flight of the Wright Brothers in 1909, it had the first golf course in Europe, opened in 1850, and it is continuing its vocation as a premier sports venue thanks to the motor racing grand prix. It is also a town full of gardens. There is the Beaumont Park with its Pyrenean Garden, the Lawrence Park, the King's Footpaths which climb steeply up between the palm trees, the park near the station reached by funicular railway, the Louis Woods, the Morlaas Boulevard and, last but not least, the Pyrenees Boulevard, a magnificent 19th-century promenade from which there is a remarkable panoramic view of the Pyrenees range, the Pic du Midi d'Ossau and the hillside vineyards that produce Jurançon.

Opposite: Pau Castle seen from the Basse-Plante, with the Mazères and Louis-Philippe Towers. The Billère Tower can just be seen on the North side.

Overleaf: the Pic du Midi d'Ossau (alt. 9,373 ft.). The Aspe Valley near the Somport Pass.

Oloron-Sainte-Marie.

Built at the confluence of the Aspe and Ossau rivers, **Oloron-Sainte-Marie** owes its charm to its geographical setting and to the historic old town (Sainte-Croix and Sainte-Marie districts). A gentle stroll will take you past buildings of considerable architectural interest. There are old houses with slate roofs, sturdy iron-studded doors with carved pediments, and the reflections of the old wool-washers' houses in the waters of the rivers.

Perched on a hilltop, Holyrood Church (Sainte-Croix) is built in a remarkable 12th-century Romanesque style. Less pure in its lines, St. Mary's Cathedral has a Romanesque doorway topped by a wonderful tympanum. It was built after a return from a Crusade and was one of the major halts along the road to Santiago de Compostela.

Memories of Gaston Phoebus still abound in the mediaeval castles at **Montaner** and **Morlanne. Coarraze**, on the other hand, is steeped in memories of Henri IV's childhood. **Orthez** is a town with character and an eventful history. It was also the brilliant capital of Béarn during the days of Gaston Phoebus. The 13th-century Moncade Tower is all that remains of its once

luxurious castle, but the town still has much to remind visitors of its prestigious history. Sights include the 16th-century house belonging to Jeanne d'Albret, the Moon private residence (15th Century) the Gothic Church of St. Peter, the old fortified bridge, the town gate etc.

Built in the 13th Century, the fortified hilltop towns of **Navarrenx, Bellocq, Sauveterre, Nay** and **Gan** have a geometric layout. They were fortified defences capable of accommodating a large population. **Bellocq**, built on the orders of Gaston VII, is the oldest of them all and it juts up from the middle of a vineyard. The fortress still has its seven crenelated towers.

Navarrenx, which was built in 1316, stretches along the banks and beaches of the Oloron river. An old bridge spans the waterway. From the top of the town walls, it is easy to see the grid pattern forming the basic urban layout.

Sauveterre keeps alive the legend of the Old Bridge. After the death of her husband, Queen Sancie gave birth to a handicapped child. She was held responsible for this ill-fortune and was severely punished. However, the

Arrens at the foot of the Pic du Gabizos (on the borders of the Hautes-Pyrénées and Pyrénées-Atlantiques).

waters of the R. Oloron into which she had been thrown carried her back up onto the bank, proving her innocence. From the beautiful Romanesque Church of St. Andrew and the mediaeval castle beyond the walls, there is an enchanting view of the Oloron river, the wooded island of La Glère and, in the distance, the Pyrenees.

The hilltop town of **Nay** was built in the 16th Century on the banks of the Pau river and it opens onto a wonderful square flanked by arcades. A quiet walk takes you to Jeanne d'Albret's Renaissance square house, to the covered market with its wonderful rafters, and to the 15th-century St. Vincent's Church. As to **Gan**, it won fame when, in 1553, Jurançon was used to christen Henri IV. **Lescar** is no longer popular with princes but, in the Middle Ages, they chose this as their capital. In the cathedral's crypt are the tombs of some of these princes i.e. François Phoebus, Catherine of Navarre, Henri d'Albret, Margaret of Angoulême etc. From its age-old history, Lescar has retained a Roman wall that has been subject to alteration over the centuries. Notre-Dame Cathedral serves as a reminder of the

town's religious importance in the Middle Ages. Its Romanesque architecture is of great interest. The chevet is flanked by radiating chapels, it has a barrel-vaulted nave, and other features of particular interest include its carvings, its choirstalls and altar screens and, more especially, its mosaics which depict hunting scenes.

There are, though, other towns in Béarn that are also worth a visit. In **Béost**, there are Renaissance houses which are unusual for their indoor bread ovens. A stroll through the streets in **Bielle, Gan, Laruns,** or **Morlaas** will given you an opportunity to admire their architectural heritage - Renaissance houses with mullioned windows, churches decorated with pink or white marble from **Arudy**, or doors and doorknockers carved with the cockle shells that symbolise Santiago de Compostela. Beyond the green rural valleys are the attractive mountain villages that form the cornerstone of the innermost soul of the Béarn people.

As you travel from town to village and on to yet another village, you will find the past opening up before your eyes in the old houses and other buildings. Follow the route to Santiago de Compostela like the pilgrims of

the Middle Ages. They set off from Vézelay, Le Puy or Paris, and travelled along three roads in France, which came together in Béarn and the Basque Country to take the pilgrims across the Pyrenees at Roncesvalles or Le Somport. In the overnight stops and hospices along the road, the pilgrims had an opportunity to rebuild their strength. It was Gaston IV who encouraged the building of these hostels and they were managed by Benedictine monks. The result is that, today in Béarn, there is a remarkable succession of Romanesque churches. Take time to visit the cathedrals in **Oloron** and **Lescar**, stop and visit the old hospices in Lacommande with their superb pictorial capitals, in **Saint-Blaise** where the domes are decidedly oriental in appearance, in **Orion** or **Peyrahere**. In Morlaas, the church which was begun in the 11th Century was then a Cluniac priory. In **Borce**, there is a stoop representing St. James and, in Orthez, there is a wonderful recumbent statue dating from the 14th Century in the Chapel of Our Lady. The church in Sauveterre, which is topped by a 13th-century belltower-keep, still has capitals dating from the transitional period between Romanesque and Gothic. Paleo-Christian sarco-phagi and pictorial capitals are the treasures in the former monastery in **Lucq-de-Béarn** while in **Sarrance** the 17th-century cloisters are of an elegance rarely seen.

The Pyrenees have much to offer sports enthusiasts - hill walking, pony trekking, rock climbing, mountaineering, skiing, hang gliding, parapente, white water rafting, canoeing, pot-holing etc. While there are many who hurtle down the ski slopes every year in **Gourette, La Pierre-Saint-Martin, Artouste, Issarbe** or **Le Somport**, there are others who prefer to go beneath the ground into the strange **Bétharram Caves**, five storeys deep, where the vastly-differing concretions are supremely beautiful.

Nature is equally impressive at the mountain passes such as **Aubisque, Pourtalet, Marie-Blanque,** or **Castet, Aste** and **Béon.**

Grazing in the wild are herds of cows, donkeys, sheep and horses, innocently motionless in the middle of the road. Nature in the Pyrenees, though, has much more to offer. The spa towns of **Les Eaux-Bonnes, Les Eaux-Chaudes, Saint-Christau,** and **Salies-de-Béarn** are ideal for relaxation and getting back into shape.

Overleaf: the Col d'Aubisque beyond Gourette at the foot of the Pic du Ger. Every summer, this grandiose landscape provides the background to the most memorable moments in the Tour de France cycle race.

Opposite: Sarrance and the cloisters, rebuilt in the 17th Century, in which Margaret of Angoulême wrote her Heptaméron.

Gourette and the Aubisque Pass.

On the road to the Col d'Aubisque.

Opposite: Franco-Spanish mountaintops near the Col du Pourtalet (top).
Waterfall and mountain stream in the Ossau Valley (bottom).

Salies is also a salt-producing town and the mines have probably been worked since the days of Antiquity. Every year, there is a Salt Festival for the locals are convinced that the mineral is highly beneficial in many different ways.

Taking a cable car ride up to the ski resort of **Artouste** from the **Lac de Fabrèges** is another of the highlights of any visit to the Béarn area of the Pyrenees. Situated at an altitude of 6,500 ft, the resort gives those who enjoy "skiing with a view" a chance to glide through an unspoilt landscape with a view over the Pic du Midi d'Ossau. During the summer, the little train in Artouste takes visitors over a distance of 6 miles through

The Fabrèges Lake and resort of Artouste.

On previous pages: The Artouste Lake.

the mountains, passing precipices and peaks until it reaches the pure clear waters of the **Lac d'Artouste**.

There is one last, gourmet, route to be taken. Thanks to local produce and a certain elegance in lifestyle, the cuisine in Béarn is varied, rich, rustic yet refined. Since Henri IV first made his famous comment about braised chicken, the menu has grown to include other appetising dishes such as the smooth *garbure*, a vegetable soup given additional taste by the inclusion of a ham bone, patés, mountain hams, sausage, chitterlings, black sausage, potted goose and duck, foie gras, wild boar stew, ring dove ragout, preserved meats, penny buns sauted with parsley, garlic and butter, salmon, and trout. Not to mention the local cheeses made from ewe's or cow's milk in the purest pastoral traditions by mountain shep-

herds and matured in the cheese cellars down in the valleys. Finally, there is the cake known as *pastis* and the doughnuts called *merveilles*. All of this washed down, of course, with a Jurançon or Madiran. Jurançon, a dry white with a brilliant yet pale robe or a sweet white with a golden robe tinted with green, is produced on 600 hectares of hillside overlooking the Pyrenees range. As soon as Henri IV was born, in 1553, he made history. Tradition has it that his grandfather "rubbed the young prince's lips with garlic and dampened his face with Jurançon". As to the Madiran reds, they are virile, fullbodied and heady, and are the ideal wine to serve with regional dishes. And to round off this list of "good local wines", there are the red, rosé and white **Béarn-Bellocq** produced between the Pau and Oloron rivers.

THE HAUTES-PYRÉNÉES

In the foothills below the Col du Tourmalet,
beyond Barèges.

The aptly-named Hautes-Pyrénées include no less than thirty-five peaks rising to an altitude of more than 9,750 ft. At an altitude of approximately 6,500 ft, the forest gives way to peaks such as **Néouvielle, Marboré, Taillon, Pic long, Arbizon, Vignemale, Balaïtous, Pic du Midi de Bigorre** etc. The landscape in the Hautes-Pyrénées provides endless sources of enjoyment, and sensations ranging from the utmost tranquillity to the absolute daring, beginning with the Tour de France cycle race. Every year, the Tour takes riders up the "Mountain Pass Route", via the **Tourmalet, Aspin, Peyresourde** or **Soulor**. Summits, peaks, glaciers, corries, and lakes are just some of the natural features that encourage people to take to the footpaths. One of them leads first of all to the **cirque de Gavarnie**, a gigantic amphitheatre of limestone cliffs. Rising in the ice-cold waters on **Mont Perdu**, the **Grande Cascade** tumbles into space down a breathtaking 1,365 ft. Gavarnie, like the corries in **Estaubé** and **Troumousse**, is a superb starting point from which to begin a range of different climbs.

From the **Col de Boucharo**, the last car park, some stiff walking will take you to the **Brèche de Roland** (9,103 ft.), **Taillon** (10,208 ft.), **the Col des Isards,** the **Pic du Marboré** (10,556 ft.), the **Mont Perdu** (10,904 ft.), the **Col du Cylindre** (9,750 ft) or the **Brèche de Tuquerouge**. It takes half-an-hour to walk up to the **astronomical observatory on the Pic du Midi de Bigorre**, at an altitude of 9,311 ft. in another part of the range. This high-altitude scientific research station brings together staff from the *Centre National de Recherches Scientifiques* and NASA and has the largest telescope in France. From the mountain peak, there is a view of the Pyrenees that is nothing short of grandiose. In the distance are the Maladeta, Taillon, and Marboré ranges high above Gavarnie, the Tarbes and Garonne Plain and even the outline of the Massif Central.

The Lac de Gaube.

The corrie at Gavarnie.

Nature is of interest wherever we are, and it fully deserves our attention. The setting up of the **Pyrenees National Park** and the **Néouvielle Nature Reserve** ensures that it will be preserved.

Beyond the winding road known as the "Squirrels', Blueberry and Edelweiss Route" are the lakes at **Orédon** and **Cap-de-Long** near the peaks at Néouvielle. There are, though, many other high-altitude lakes scattered throughout the mountains, and they are an inevitable feature of any walk. From the **Pont d'Espagne**, it takes only ten minutes to walk up to the superb **Lac de Gaubeor** you may prefer to take the skilift and walk only the last few yards. Equally outstanding are the lakes named **Bleu, d'Estaing, Ossoue, Labas, Estom-Soubiran,** and **Gentianes.**

The water is a source of admiration on the surface but it is also acknowledged in the bowels of the earth where it undertakes its long, patient work of erosion. The five-storey **Bétharram Caves** consist of a labyrinth of galleries, and chambers full of stalagmites or hung with stalactites in many different shapes - a giant bell, a minaret, a fortress, a man's head, or the outline of a rhinoceros. Visitors go down to a depth of some 260 ft. during the tour until they reach the underground river where a small-gauge railway waits to bring them back to the mouth of the cave.

The village of Gavarnie.

Scenery in the area around the Col du Boucharo (top).

The Latour Valley near Cauterets (right).

Opposite: the pic du Midi de Bigorre.

Overleaf: the lake at Cap-de-Long (alt. 7,020 ft.) in the shadow of the Trois Conseillers (9,877 ft.), Néouvielle (10,049 ft.) and Ramougn (9,786 ft.).

The caves at **Médous** (near Bagnères-de-Bigorre), **Le Loup, Les Sarrasins, Béout** and **Le Pic de Jer** (near Lourdes) are also open to the public.

Equally famous for its health-giving properties, water is admired for three different aspects of its existence. The Hautes-Pyrénées' has been known for its spas since time immemorial. The Gallo-Romans knew about the benefits of thermal baths. The *tepidarium* (tepid bath), the *caldarium* (the hot bath), and the *frigidarium* (cold bath) were very popular places in which to get back into shape and meet people. In **Bagnères-de-Bigorre**, the discovery of an ancient bath made of pink marble has proved the town's age-old vocation as a spa. Since the Middle Ages, many a celebrity has brought fame to the spa towns, among them Montaigne, Rabelais, Margaret of Navarre, and Empress Eugénie. Nowadays, **Argelès-**

Top to bottom, and left to right:
Les Sarradets at the foot of Roland's Breach.

Roland's Breach (9,123 ft.), on the French side of the border.

Roland's Breach on the Spanish side of the border.

The "Doigt" (literally, "the Finger").

The refuge on Les Sarradets overlooked by the Tower and the Helmet.

The refuge and mountain at Les Sarradets at the foot of Roland's Breach.

Opposite: Roland's Breach on the French side of the border.

Gazost, Bagnères-de-Bigorre, Barèges, Beaucens, Capvern-les-Bains, Cauterets, Luz-Saint-Sauveur, and **Saint-Lary** provide a wide range of treatments such as jacuzzis, massages, saunas, Turkish baths etc, all of them designed to get patients back into tiptop shape.

Healthy leisure activities are not restricted to the winter months. With hill walking in the summer and winter sports in thirteen different resorts, the mountain range is a wonderful place for pure air and enjoyment. The pistes at **La Mongie, Saint-Lary, Piau-Engaly, Barèges, Luz-Ardiden, Cauterets,** and **Val d'Ouron** cling to the tallest peaks in the Pyrenees.

Surrounded by this high-quality natural environment, the local people have a deep-seated love of their region, which they also call "Bigorre". It could, perhaps, hardly be otherwise. But the history of the County of Bigorre, with its capital, Tarbes, is very complex. This was one of the largest fiefs in Gascony and was much cove-

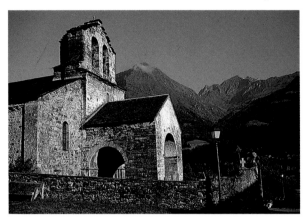

The church in Sère near Luz-Saint-Sauveur.

ted by the English. It was annexed to the Crown of France in 1607 but, in the meantime, had succeeded in maintaining its status as an independent, sovereign State in the same way as Béarn.

Opposite: The observatory and television mast on the Pic du Midi de Bigorre (alt. 9,311 ft.).

The ski resort of La Mongie, a vast area at altitudes ranging from 5,687 ft. to 7,800 ft. Taken with the resort of Barèges, it provides skiers with more than 60 miles of pistes.

A pilgrimage in Lourdes.

La Mongie.

On 11th February 1858, the Virgin Mary appeared to a child named Bernadette Soubirous, making the Hautes-Pyrénées, and Lourdes where the miracle occured, one of the world's main places of pilgrimage.

If it is architectural heritage that interests you, then the best place to start your tour of Bigorre is in **Tarbes**. Despite its geographical situation on the plain, the town resolutely faces the mountains. The Massey Gardens in the town centre form a vast English-style park boasting a number of rare botanic specimens. The stud set up by Napoleon I during the Franco-Spanish War is well worth

Lourdes Castle.

Overleaf: Oredon Lake.

a visit, as are Maréchal Foch's birthplace, the Sède Cathedral, the Collegiate Church of St. John, the Hussards Museum and the Massey Museum.

In the foothills of the Pyrenees beside the R. Pau, lies **Lourdes**, which has been one of the most famous places of pilgrimage in the Christian world for the past century. On 11th February 1858, the Virgin Mary appeared to Bernadette Soubirous eighteen times in the Massabielle Cave. The child reported the words She spoke, "I am the Immaculate Conception". After being declared authentic by the Roman Catholic Church, the events were followed by a number of miracle cures. From then on, pilgrims from all over the world arrived in the town, in increasing numbers. The **underground St. Pius X Basilica** is one of the largest churches in the world and can cater for a congregation of 25,000. The **Stations of the Cross** and the **Rosary Basilica** are other places of prayer. **Lourdes Castle**, dating from the 16th and 17th Centuries, stands on the top of a spur of rock 260 ft. high. Since 1920, it has housed a Pyrenean Museum specialising in costume, folklore and traditional arts and crafts.

THE PYRENEES IN HAUTE-GARONNE

Every area of the mountain provides a generous supply of water.

Haute-Garonne is a *département* with two faces but only the southern area is of interest to us. In the centre and the North, the R. Garonne flows through wide alluvial plains down to Toulouse while in the South the Pyrenees change the landscape and the everyday life of the inhabitants. From the **France Hospice** near Luchon, a walk of only a few hours will take you to the **Port de Vénasque**, a mountain pass close to the highest peaks in the range. You can see the **Pic d'Aneto** (11,076 ft.) flanked by the **Maladeta** (10,751 ft.), and the **Mulleres** (9,782 ft.). At the foot of the mountains you can see the waters of the young Garonne, rushing and tumbling into the **Trou du Toro**. The mountain lakes, filled with crystal clear waters and, in some cases such as **Boum**, flowing from waterfall to cascade, are found after several hours' walking. Hillwalkers, with rucksack and the appropriate clothing, follow the stony, and sometimes very steep, paths up to the **Lac d'Oo**, a lake covering an area of 38 hectares at an altitude of 4,888 ft. Higher still is the **Lac d'Espingo** flowing into Oo via a waterfall 887 ft. high.

The France Hospice (right).

Opposite: Beyond the Port de Vénasque, there is an incomparable view of the Maladeta range and the Pic d'Aneto.

Setting off for the Port de Vénasque.

From the ski resort of **Superbagnères**, there is always a wonderful view of the surrounding mountain tops. Winter and summer alike, the charm remains the same. Those who enjoy spending time in a natural environment will also like **Peyregaudes, Bourg-d'Oueil** and **Les Agudes**, the main ski resorts with Superbagnères.

It is not unusual, in this area, to find more of the mineral springs that are so common throughout the Pyrenees. **Luchon** (its official name is Bagnères-de-Luchon) is the most popular spa town in France in terms of numbers of visitors. Built at the confluence of the One and Pique rivers, it stretches along the floor of a tree-filled valley, watched over by the tallest peaks in the range. Because of this, it is an ideal starting point for climbers and hillwalkers. Luchon has almost eighty springs providing water with high sulphur, iron and calcium sulphate contents tapped high up in the mountains. It has retained something of the charm of the spa town that it was during the 1930's, and has many buildings dating from this period. The old town of Luchon huddles round the church and is reminiscent of a Pyrenean village. The main thoroughfare is the avenue known as the Allées d'Etigny, named after an Intendant of Gascony who did much to develop Luchon in the 18th Century. It leads to the vast pump rooms at the end of the Parc des Quinconces. The nearby Allée des Bains leads to the casino.

The other thermal springs in Haute-Garonne are to be found in the resorts of **Barbazan** and **Salies-de-Salat**.

The history of **Saint-Gaudens**, the main town in the Comminges area, revolves around the life of a 13-year-old shepherd boy who, in the 5th Century, preferred to die rather than renounce his Christian faith. His name was Gaudens and he was beheaded by Roman soldiers. The Romanesque chapel of La Caoue and Montjoie stand on the spot where the shepherd boy was beheaded. Although it has been established beyond all doubt that the town existed in the days of Antiquity, it was not until the 9th Century that a real urban community grew up around the church. This was followed by a period of outstanding Romanesque architecture producing wonders such as the collegiate church and its cloisters.

On previous pages: Before crossing the Port de Vénasque, coming from the direction of the France Hospice, remember to look back and enjoy the majestic sight of the Boum Lakes incrusted like gemstones in the mountains.

Bagnères-de-Luchon.

Topped by a tower with countless semi-rounded openings, the design of the collegiate church was largely based on the Church of St. Sernin in Toulouse. Inside, there is a 12th-century nave and superb pictorial capitals. The galleries, choirstalls, 17th-century Aubusson tapestries and organ are the main features in the ornate interior. The church is also famous for having the largest peal of bells in the Midi-Pyrénées region. Next to the church stand the cloisters, which were partially destroyed in the 19th Century. They too were fine examples of Romanesque architecture, decorated with capitals bearing a variety of carvings. As in Pau, the Boulevard des Pyrénées in Saint-Gaudens is a delightful promenade from which there is a panoramic view stretching over a distance of 112 miles, from the mountains in Ariège to the Pic du Midi.

Near Saint-Gaudens, in **Montmaurin**, the remains of a vast Gallo-Roman villa were uncovered in 1947. The prehistoric rock shelters in the **Gorges de la Save** seem to suggest that the Comminges area is also one of the cradles of humanity.

While on the subject of masterpieces of Romanesque architecture, we must mention the 11th-century Church of **Saint-Just-de-Valcabrère**. The North door is topped by a tympanum and four marble statues. Inside, there are pictorial capitals, ancient columns, and Gallo-Roman decoration set into the walls. **Saint-Aventin**, which dates from the Early Romanesque period, has carved bas-reliefs that are fine examples of 11th-Century Languedoc-style art.

Let us go on down through the centuries and along the road to **Saint-Bertrand-de-Comminges**, standing on a hilltop overlooking the R. Garonne. The town was first founded in 72 B.C. but did not really begin to develop until the 9th Century, thanks to the Bishop of Comminges, St. Bertrand. He it was who commissioned the building of the cathedral we see today, and this, in turn, gave the local people stability, laying the bases for a new town. Notre-Dame Cathedral is a majestic building containing Romanesque remains (door, first span in the nave), and Gothic sections (apse and nave). The furnishings are rich and ornate - pulpit, organ loft and Renais-

The spa town of Luchon.

sance choirstalls, altar screen, and a High Altar made of Pyrenean marble. There is also a roodscreen and stained glass windows dating from the 16th Century.

Nearby, in the Romanesque cloisters, are rows of Gallo-Roman sarcophagi, capitals and pillars carved with the figures of the Evangelists. In the former Benedictine monastery, the Trophy Gallery housed in a small chapel contains a collection of statues dating from the 1st and 2nd Centuries, just some of the treasures found in Saint-Bertrand-de-Comminges.

Montréjeau, at the confluence of the Neste and Garonne rivers, (its name means "royal mountain") also grew up on the sheer sides of a spur of rock. It is a fortified hilltop town with the traditional layout of streets set at right angles to each other, a central square flanked by arcades, mediaeval houses etc.

If you follow the course of the R. Garonne to **Saint-Martory,** you will see a 18th-century bridge flanked by

Even at high altitudes, animal and plant life and minerals are still easy to see.

two gates before you enter the town itself. Little remains of the 13th-century cloisters that were once part of **Bonnefon Abbey** but **Montpezat Castle** (part 15th and 16th Centuries) still stands proudly intact.

Haute-Garonne turns over the pages of its history book slowly, musing over its architectural heritage and its natural environment, as you go from road to track to footpath - and everything is well worth taking time to see. After a long walk, too, you can sit back and enjoy the excellent food served in the Pyrenees, knowing that Haute-Garonne boasts a particularly generous table. The brotherhood known as the **"Tasto-Moujetos du Comminges"** ensures that the humble bean forming the main ingredient in many of the dishes and providing such a wonderful accompaniment to lamb, pork and duck is never forgotten. But this should not prevent you from tasting the salt leg of pork, tripe cooked in a number of different ways, and the goat's cheeses made in the mountains, all of them other local delicacies.

THE PYRENEES IN ARIÈGE

*In Olbier near Vicdessos, beneath the few remaining ruins
of the castle of Montréal-de-Sos, there is a cave containing an illustration
of the Holy Grail.*

The two historical areas in Ariège, Couserans and the County of Foix, had very little contact with each other over the centuries. But they were as close in geographical terms as they were distant in historical destiny.

The **Couserans** area was dominated by religious influences and was always strongly attached to Roman Catholicism. It was well-known for its inclination towards Aquitaine, if only for its use of the Gascon language. The **County of Foix**, on the other hand, was a powerful feudal entity established c. 1,000 A.D. and it had a totally different outlook. It tended to turn towards Toulouse and the Mediterranean, and it was the language of Languedoc that was spoken here. It was an area favourable to the new ideas of **Catharism** and Protestantism, and religion left its mark on both the population and the architecture. The dazzling destiny of the County of Foix far outshone the history of Couserans. From the days of the Albigensian Crusade to the setting up of the great Pyrenean State of Foix-Béarn by Gaston Phoebus and Henri of Navarre, its history was both eventful and thrilling. Couserans and County of Foix were united in 1789 by the Constituant Assembly but there was a marked lack of enthusiasm at grass roots level. Nowadays, though, Ariège seems to have achieved a sense of unity, around its modest main town, Foix.

The land in Ariège is difficult to cultivate, the climate is hard, and there is a long-standing tradition of livestock farming. However, underground the area conceals untold riches. Among them are the caves at **Niaux, le Mas d'Azil** and **Bédeilhac** whose walls bear moving reminders of prehistoric art forms. As to the caves in **Lombrives** and **Labouiche**, they conceal a fairy-tale world of natural concretions.

Niaux is world-famous and has fascinated even the greatest of prehistory experts. Situated near Tarascon-sur-Ariège, its galleries stretch over a distance of several miles. On the limestone walls are bison, horses, stags, and mountain goats sketched in black and surrounded by enigmatic symbols painted in red and black. The almost life-sized horse known as the "Bearded Horse of the Pyrenees" is reminiscent of the pottoks we see in the mountains today. The main chamber in the

Opposite: Life on the land demands steadfast courage.

The ibex in the Black Chamber in the Niaux cave.
This painting was created during the Magdalanian Era some 14,000 years ago. Photo by R. Robert.

The Romanesque church in Saint-Jean-des-Verges.

cave is the "Black Lounge" decorated with drawings dating back to the Magdalanian Era. Wall paintings, engravings, and footprints are among the other features of the cave, and they are kept safe within galleries that are closed to the public.

The cave at **Le Mas d'Azil** was used by a whole range of animals that sought shelter here long before Man. Bones of mammoths, bears and rhinoceros have been found here, dating from the Paleolithic Age. Over the centuries, the cave has served as a refuge for many different people (hence its name, "asile" in French means "sanctuary"). Originally, the Magdalanian and, later, the peoples of the Mesolithic Age (known as "Azilians") created carvings and engravings, leaving pictures of birds, reindeer etc. on the walls of the cave and on contemporary objects. Some outstanding artefacts and tools form the basis of the rich collections built up from finds made in the cave. Later, persecuted groups such as early Christians, Cathars, and Huguenots took refuge here. Now, the cave is one of the most important prehistoric sites in the world.

The vast cave at **Bédeilhac** lies beyond a monumental porch carved out of the Sédour Rock. It is a gigantic

cave and is easy to reach. It has been in frequent use by man over the centuries, from the Paleolithic Age to the 20th Century. Paintings, drawings and engravings have been preserved here for fourteen thousand years.

The impressive cave in **Lombrives** deserves a special mention for two main reasons i.e. its sheer size makes it the largest cave in Europe and it has a legend attached to it that is said to have given rise to the name "Pyrenees". 'Tis a tale worth telling. During one of his travels, Hercules visited the palace of King Bebrix and fell in love with his daughter, Pyrene. She died in a tragic accident, having been swallowed up in the cave at Lombrives before Hercules could save her. In memory of his lost love, Hercules called the surrounding mountains, "Pyrenees".

From Cathar castle to Romanesque church, religion has overstepped the boundaries of the dramatic events instigated in its name to create truly wonderful buildings. Between the 10th and 12th Centuries, Romanesque architecture spread throughout the valleys of Ariège, leaving its mark on many of the churches. In some cases, the architectural style is pure and unadulterated, as in **Saint-Jean-des-Verges**, one of the most beautiful churches in Ariège. The influence of nearby Catalonia can be seen in the churches in **Mérens, Ornolac,** and **Vernaux** and in the cloisters in **Saint-Lizier**, while **Unac, Axiat and Miglos** are more Andorran in style. **Ourjout, Castillon, Montgauch,** and **Antras** in Couserans are covered with Spanish decoration. **Saint-Jean-des-Verges, Unac, Mercuz, Daumazan, Sainte-Suzanne,** and **Villeneuve-du-Latou** are reminiscent of the Toulouse School for their profusion of carvings. As to **Notre-Dame-de-Luzenac, Niaux, Pamiers** and **Erce**, they are partly Romanesque and have wonderful doors, belltowers or apses. Some of the churches, e.g. in **Vals, Saint-Lizier** and **Montgauch** are fortunate enough to have kept their brightly-coloured frescoes.

Although the historical heart of the Cathar area is the *département* of Aude, the centre of the new religion that was born in the 12th Century was in Ariège, in **Montségur**. **Foix, Lordat, Miglos, Roquefixade, Usson and Montaillou** were all to know religious fervour and, later, dramatic events. At the end of the 12th Century, Occitania was a prosperous region, along whose roads travelled merchants from countless different countries. The Counts of Toulouse and Foix governed in a climate of

The ruins of the castle in Montaillou.

tolerance, freedom and open-mindedness. Because of this, the new ideas of the Cathar religion were given a favourable hearing in the area. They arrived just when the excesses of the Roman Catholic Church, with its wealth and its Crusades to the Holy Land, were beginning to arouse considerable controversy. The **Cathars** were Christians who based their religious practices on Christ and the Gospels. But their concept of religion

The ruins of Roquefixade Castle are difficult to distinguish from the surrounding countryside.

The ruins of Lordat Castle.

Opposite: the "pog" at Montségur (top) and Fort Usson in Rouze (bottom).

On previous pages: Miglos, a 12th-14th Century castle whose owner was a Cathar lord.

was totally different to anything that had gone before. Theirs was a manicheistic doctrine that rejected the Catholic idea of a single God. They questioned the role of priests, the Pope and some of the sacraments as intermediaries. There was no supreme chief in this religion and beliefs were handed down to the faithful by "Perfects", men and women who were all considered as equals and were baptised. The Cathars believed in reincarnation and forced themselves to tell the truth at all times. They undertook a search for spiritual purity, were profound pacifists, and were almost total vegetarians. They believed in giving charity and remained poor themselves. The exemplary nature of their lifestyle drew in more and more believers.

Faced with the threat to the Roman Catholic Church, the Pope and clergy, terrified by what they saw, declared the Cathars to be anti-clerical heretics. Thereafter, a Holy War was launched against them, lasting from 1209 to 1229. This "Albigensian" Crusade led to

persecution of a violence rarely seen and ended with the Cathars being burnt at the stake.

Montségur Castle is an eagle's nest perched at the top of a rock known as a "pog" (alt. 3,922 ft.) and is the symbol of Catharism. For reasons of security and with a view to uplifting the souls of believers, the Cathar fortresses were all built on peaks that were difficult to reach. Today, it still takes effort and energy to walk up to Montségur and pass through the South Gate. Beyond the gate is the inner courtyard, the small keep, and the remains of a barbican and look-out post. Montségur, a ruined citadel that nevertheless remains impressive, has always been steeped in mystery. The direction of its layout has raised a number of questions after a historian noticed that, on 21st June, the day of the summer solstice, the first rays of the sun passed through the slit windows in the keep. Some would have you believe that the Cathars' treasure trove was buried there; others that the treasure is, in fact, the Holy Grail. After a ten-month siege supported by Hugues

des Arcis at the head of an army of six thousand men, Montségur finally fell in March 1244. An enormous fire was built on the *Champ des Brûlés* (the Field of those burnt at the stake) where a commemorative stele stands today. Two hundred and twenty-five Cathars, who refused to abjure their faith, threw themselves into the flames, carrying their greatest secrets away with them.

Lordat, which lay too high up in the mountains, escaped the Crusade. Now part of the County of Foix, it has a keep and the remains of its three outer walls. The fortress in **Usson** still has a tall, pentagonal keep surrounded by walls now lying in ruins. **Montaillou** is a heap of windswept ruins. **Roquefixade** is reminiscent of Montségur and stands at the top of a spur of rock. With a bit of imagination, you can pick out the remains of a keep, the outer wall, and the courtyard among the ruins. **Miglos Castle** is now nothing but a collection of impressive walls; its owner was a Cathar Lord. A square keep and rectangular apartments built in the 14th Century can still be seen.

Foix is the main town in Ariège and it provides a wonderful history lesson. The **mediaeval castle** is the symbol of the town as a whole, rising to a height of more than195 ft. Successive Counts of Foix lived there, defending the Cathar faith like many other noblemen in the South of France. Foix escaped the destruction threatened by Simon de Montfort, despite Count Raymond Roger's known support for Catharism. The celebrated Gaston Phoebus also stayed in the castle whose origins date back to the 10th Century. Three tall keeps now jut up above the walls, all that remain of a castle that was once much larger. The Ariège Museum housed in one of the wings has collections of exhibits dating back to prehistoric, Roman and mediaeval times, and an engraving of a fish from the Cathar period.

At the foot of the castle is the old town of Foix, which is carefully maintaining its mediaeval appearance with timbered houses, cobbled streets, and small squares. Every year, the local people dress up as knights, squires, gentle ladies and simple country bumpkins, creating a colourful historical atmosphere throughout the Festival Period.

Of all the natural features of Ariège, mineral springs hold pride of place. **Ax-les-Thermes**, where the supply

Foix and its castle.

Mirepoix.

Pamiers and its cathedral.

of sulphur-bearing water seems to be endless, has specialised in the treatment of rheumatism and respiratory infections. **Ussat-les-Bains** and **Aulus-les-Bains** are as much spa towns as holiday centres.

Ariège is a land with a history, a *département* in which unpretentious rural communities have a charm that is little short of touching. **Pamiers**, where red predominates thanks to the use of brick, still remembers its abbey founded in the 11th Century, but the only reminder of its actual existence is a Romanesque doorway, now integrated into the Gothic architecture of St. Antonin's Cathedral. The hilltop village of **Mirepoix**, with its fine central square surrounded by arcades, its mediaeval half-timbered houses and its huge cathedral, dates from the 13th Century. The original town of Mirepoix, which ardently supported the Cathar religion, disappeared in 1279 in a terrible flood.

Wherever you go, from **Tarascon** to **Saverdun**, and from **Saint-Lizier** to **Mirepoix**, local fare is sure to satisfy your appetite. There is trout fished in mountain streams, duck fillets with morels or penny buns, Ariège's own *cassoulet* (a bean stew with preserved duck), tripe stew in the County of Foix, chicken drumstick with traditional stuffing... Whatever the dish, it delights those with a fine palate and those with a large appetite.

THE PYRÉNÉES-ORIENTALES

Coumasse Lake near Font-Romeu.

The old province of Roussillon corresponds more or less to the *département* of Pyrénées-Orientales. From the **Col de Puymorens** to the Mediterranean, the mountains of Catalonia slope and plunge down into the sea. First of all, you will see the tall peaks of the Pyrenees i.e. the **Carlit** (9,493 ft.), **Puigmal** (9,454 ft.), and **Canigou** (9,051 ft.) then the foothills of the **Capcir, Cerdagne, Conflent** and **Vallespir** areas followed by the **Albères** range where the rocks are bare and hard, and the climate already drier and hotter. These outcrops of the Pyrenees eventually reach the **Vermillion Coast** where creeks conceal towns such as Cerbère, Banyuls, Port-Vendres and Collioure. Further North is the Roussillon Plain, and **Perpignan**. Here the rock-strewn coast that twists and winds from Cerbère to Collioure gives way to sandy beaches from Argelès onwards.

Situated at the junction of major historical overland routes, in a place where Nordic and Mediterranean cultures and people come together, Roussillon has always been a land of travellers, occupying forces and political jealousy. Long before the Celts, the Iberians, the Carthaginians or the Romans came here, it had been chosen by prehistoric man for his settlements. In one of the cliffs surrounding the village of **Tautavel** is a cave, the "Caune d'Arago" which gave the world a priceless treasure. On 22nd July 1971, a skull belonging to *homo erectus* was uncovered here; it is now known to be the oldest skull in Europe (450,000 years B.C).

By the time the Romans settled in Roussillon, "Portus Veneris" (Port-Vendres) which had been founded by the Phoenicians in the 6th Century B.C. had already been in existence for some long time. Spurred on by the prosperity acquired from trade, people began to set up small, but dynamic, harbours to each side of the town. Goods were carried inland via Cerbère and the Col du Perthus. Among the most highly-sought goods, there was one for which the Catalan people have to thank the Romans - wine. Of all the plants currently grown in Roussillon, whether orchard fruits or vegetables, there is no doubt that the vines take pride of place, as well as being the oldest form of agriculture locally. As Pliny the Elder said, the people of Ancient Greece and Rome very soon grew to appreciate the drink. Vines were a major preoccupation of the Romans, and are the subject of carvings on the 7th-century stone coffins seen in the **cloisters in Elne.**

Collioure, the place where the locals keep "one foot in their vineyard and one foot on their boat".

A major road, the "**Via Domitia**" running from Perthus to Beaucaire in the *département* of Gard, was laid out in 188 B.C. by Gnaeus Domitius. To the East, it ran along the coast (from Banyuls to Perpignan); further inland, it ran through the **gorges.** An outstanding set of border fortifications can still be seen there. Two fortresses stand high above the "Via Domitia". To the East of Perpignan, the road ran alongside the hillfort discovered at **Ruscino.**

Once the invasions by the Visigoths and the Saracen had ended, **Cerdagne** and **Roussillon** were administered by Frankish Counts. In the 12th Century, the last of their line bequeathed their fiefs to Alfonso II of Aragon. Thereafter, the destiny of Roussillon was closely linked to that of Spanish Catalonia. Perpignan underwent major development and became the capital of the Kings of Majorca. The fortress in **Salses**, which was designed to monitor movements along the border, did nothing to quench the inevitable French desire to reconquer the territory. Roussillon was lost and recaptured on countless occasions until, with the signing of the **Treaty of the Pyrenees** in 1659, it finally became French again. Despite this, it retained certain rights and its own particular character, which had been forged after years of contact with a Hispanic civilisation.

The **sardana,** which was partially prohibited in Spain during the Franco years, is both music and dance and it carries with it all that Catalan culture has to offer. Played and danced on both sides of the Pyrenees, it is the subject of meetings and competitions in which each *coble* defends its title. A sardana competition is a strictly-organised event, in both form and content. Each group dances a number of figures and is awarded marks by a jury. It is a discipline that involves fitness, artistic ability and cultural knowledge and it seems to bear within it the very essence of the Catalans, viz. hidden emotions. The festival held in **Céret** in the summer includes one of the best opportunities to watch the sardana. Men and women move round the arena, hand in hand, forming long, concentric circles that create a moving chain of friendship. They dance to the unusual sounds of the *cobla* (the orchestra) consisting of flaviole, shawm, tabale, and prima.

In the Pyrénées-Orientales, the altitude rises from sea-level on the shores of the Mediterranean up to 9,493 ft. at the highest peak, the **Carlit**. High up in the mountains,

Overleaf: The hearts of all Catalan people are set alight by the rhythm of the sardana. Here it is being performed in the bullfighting ring at Céret, at the foot of the Canigou.

The Devil's Bridge (14th Century) in Céret.

In the Font-Romeu area, Mother Nature weaves her magical spells in winter and summer alike, so that every instant brings a sense of well-being and relaxation.

Opposite: Vive Lake near Font-Romeu (top),
Llat Lake (centre),
Lac des Bouillouses
(bottom left and bottom right).

the vast areas available to skiers in **Capcir** and **Cerdagne** stretch over a distance of more than 62 miles around the resorts of **Font-Romeu, Les Angles, Formiguères, Bolquères Pyrénées 2000** and **Puigmal**. The pistes that run through alpine pastures and forests are wonderful for skiers, and the whole area is ideal for mountaineers or anybody with a passion for the more dangerous sports such as canyoning, white water rafting, parapente, or pot holing. The superb natural concretions in the cave at **Fontrabious** and the hundreds of lakes (**Les Angles, Bouillouses, Lanous, Camporeils** etc.) are a delight for hillwalkers. The Lac des Bouillousses is protected by a preservation order. The area covers 1,800 hectares, lies at an altitude of 6,848 ft. and includes a number of large and small lakes (**Coumasse, Llat, Vive** etc).

In this mountainous area, Romanesque and Baroque architecture was extraordinarily popular in churches and other religious buildings. The frescoes in **Angoustrine** and **Caldegas**, and the churches in **Estavar, Iravals, Llo, Planes, Odeillo** and **Hix** all bear the hallmarks of the Romanesque period. As to the altar screens in the **Hermitage in Font-Romeu, Saint-Romain-de-Caldegas, and Sainte-Eugénie-de-Saillagousse**, they form the Baroque decoration of typical 17th-century furnishings.

From the Middle Ages to the 20th Century, the area has acquired a number of unusual pieces of architecture. The first **solar oven** built in Mont-Louis in 1953 was used as a prototype to overcome any difficulties prior to the building of the second oven in **Odeillo**, near Font-Romeu. The reason why Font-Romeu is the world's leading solar energy centre is that the sun has several exceptional advantages in the Cerdagne area. Not only are there 2,500 to 2,700 hours of sunshine per year; the rays are also particularly strong. The solar oven in Odeillo, which became operational in 1970, is now still the most powerful of its kind anywhere in the world, and it remains an irreplaceable instrument for scientific research. It houses the *Institut de Science et de Génie des Matériaux et Procédés* (Institute of Materials and Process Science and Engineering), the laboratory of the *Centre National de la Recherche Scientifique* (National Scientific Research Laboratory). The Institute's main task is research, the enhancement of new developments, and training through research, in the field of high-temperature techniques. The main areas of research carried out at the solar oven installation concern the development of ceramic materials, the study of their behaviour at high temperatures, and the development of new procedures for use in the metal-working and energy industries. The 1,000-kilowatt solar oven with its 32,280 sq. ft. of mirrors distributed between 63 heliostats and its huge 21,520 sq. ft. concentrator enable scientists to obtain temperatures of more than 3,000 °C and to bring them to bear on objects of semi-industrial size.

The Pyrénées-Orientales form a border region and they were the subject of dispute between several major kingdoms very early on in their history. Because of this, the area has a wide range of military architecture built over the centuries - from Roman hillfort to walled mediaeval towns and 17th-century fortresses. **Mont-Louis** is one of the finest examples of such military architecture. It was designed by Vauban in the 17th Century with a view to blocking the entrance to Cerdagne. The

Opposite: the fortress of Mont-Louis.

The solar oven in Odeillo.

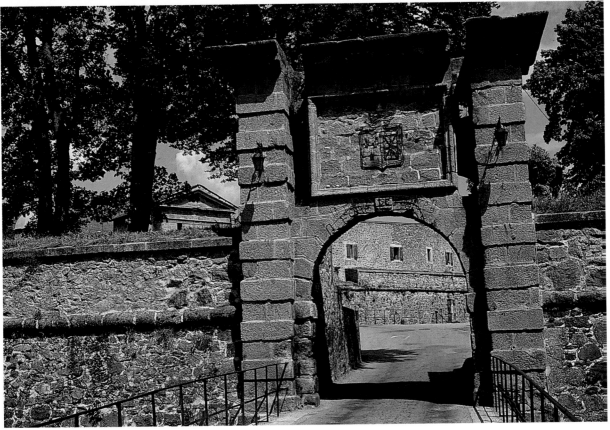

town lies entirely within walls and is the highest fortress in France, at an altitude of 5,200 ft. Overlooking it from even further up the mountainside is another fort that is Army property.

More fortresses can be seen in the Piemonts formed by the **Conflent, Vallespir** and **Aspre Valleys**. It was also Vauban who designed the **fortress in Amélie-les-Bains**. The town is a spa and is now well-known for the treatment of rheumatism and respiratory disorders. The superb walled towns of **Prats-de-Mollo, Villefranche-de-Conflent,** and **Castelnou,** the castle in **Montalba** and the fortress in **Bellegarde-du-Perthus** all do honour to their ingenious builders, each of whom had an undoubted sense of aesthetic style.

The architectural heritage in the Piemonts consists mainly of abbeys. **Sainte-Marie** in Arles-sur-Tech, the **Serrabone Priory** in Bouleternère and **Saint-Génis-des-Fontaines** are all outstanding examples of Romanesque architecture. All roads, though, lead to the most prestigious of all churches - **Saint-Michel-de-Cuxa, Saint-Martin-du-Canigou, Palalda, Conat, Corneilla-de-Conflent, Marcevol, Maureillas, Saint-André-de-Sorède** etc. The Gothic and Baroque periods seem to have been less prodigal with their bequests, but there are, nevertheless, a number of very fine buildings in **Prats-de-Mollo, Arles-sur-Tech, Boule-d'Amont, Rigarda, Vinça, Prades** etc.

From the **yellow narrow-gauge railway** linking Villefranche-de-Conflent and Latour-de-Carol, a distance of 39 miles, there is plenty of time to admire the Pyrenean countryside and its bridges e.g. the **Séjourné Viaduct,** or **the Gisclard Bridge**.

The spa towns of **Amélie-les-Bains, Le Boulou, Molitg, Prats-de-Mollo** and **Vernet-les-Bains** all boast delightful natural settings and are all ideal for anybody in search of a quiet holiday and a chance to relax. Near

Opposite: Villefranche-de-Conflent. Its 11th and 15th-century fortifications were included in a major system of defence by Vauban (top). Lost in the silence of the Aspres area stands Serrabone Priory, an outstanding example of Romanesque architecture (bottom).

Amélie-les-Bains.

Prats-de-Mollo and its church with crenelated belltower.

Corneilla-de-Conflent, take time to visit the two **Canalettes Caves** or to admire the wonderful scenery in the **Gorges de la Fou, le Mondony,** or **La Massane**.

The coastal towns of **Cerbère, Banyuls, Port-Vendres,** and **Collioure** are rather more Pyrenean for the purposes of local government and administrative red tape than as regards their geographical setting. Although the soul of a true Catalan can still be detected near the tallest peaks (some distance away), the towns are not surrounded only by the final outcrop of the **Albères**. The town of **Cerbère** nestles in the shelter of creeks near the Spanish border, as do all the other picturesque harbours. On the slopes of the last foothills of the Pyrenees are the vineyards that made **Banyuls** famous, overlooking the Mediterranean and drifting attractively down the hillsides. They extend as far as **Collioure**, the cradle of Modern Art, the town that was once home to Matisse, Derain, Dufy and Gris. From the

coast road, there is a view over the bay and its jetty, the old walled town and the projecting outline of the Church of Our Lady of Angels whose belltower served as a lighthouse in days gone by. The royal castle, one of Roussillon's lookout posts, was the former summer residence of the Kings of Majorca. If you take the steeply-sloping road to the **Madeloc Observation Platform** you will see, at an altitude of 2,060 ft, a **tower** of the same name dating from the 14th Century. The view is magnificent. It stretches right along the Vermillion Coast and across the Roussillon Plain.

We cannot leave this trip through the Pyrénées-Orientales without a mention for its main town, **Perpignan**, which is quite happy to merely catch a glimpse of the **Canigou** and the other peaks on the horizon, in the distance. Four main buildings serve as reminders of the town's historical importance. **St. John's Cathedral** is one of the finest examples of Southern French Gothic. It

Overleaf: the Benedictine Abbey of Saint-Martin-du-Canigou was built from 1001 onwards, on a spur of rock at an altitude of 3,555 ft.

Opposite: the Abbey of Saint-Michel-de-Cuxa, founded in 883 A.D, reached a peak of prosperity and influence in the 10th to 12th Centuries before falling into oblivion, and being subjected to pillaging and partial demolition.

Banyuls.

Perpignan: the Palace of the Kings of Majorca (top and bottom right) and the Castillet (bottom left).

has a wide nave and no side aisles. The most beautiful parts of its decoration are the altar screens. The **Palace of the Kings of Majorca** has dominated the town since the 13th Century, when Perpignan was a brilliant capital. The brick-built **Castillet Castle** is really a fortified gateway, all that remains of the mediaeval town walls. It now houses the **Casa Pairial**, a museum of Catalan popular arts, crafts and traditions. In the heart of the town stands the **Loge de la Mer**, once the stock exchange. Built in 1397, it is a uniform building in the Flamboyant Gothic style. Other sights will meet your eye as you stroll through the streets - the town hall built between the 13th and 17th Centuries, the 15th-century Palace of the Deputation, the Julia Residence, or the townhouses in the Rue du Théâtre, and the Rue des Marchands.

In the Pyrénées-Orientales, there is much to sustain the mind - and just as much to feed the body. From the shores of the Mediterranean to the slopes of the Canigou, the orchards supply apricots, peaches, nectarines, cherries, apples and pears. Duck with fruit is a skilful combination of sweet and sour. The *boles de picoulat, ollada, cargolade,* or *anchoïade* in Collioure, the mountain ham with honey, and sweets such as *rousquilles, bunyettes* and *tourrons* make eating in Roussillon a delightful experience. From aperitif to dessert, the area also has a rich, varied selection of wines. The **appellation d'origine contrôlée** wines e.g. the Banyuls, Collioure, Rivesaltes, Muscat de Rivesaltes, Maury, and Côtes du Roussillon form the basis of a Wine Trail that is well worth travelling along.

THE PRINCIPALITY OF ANDORRA

A small country nestling in the heart of the Pyrenees.

The principality of Andorra is a small country in the heart of the Pyrenees, between France and Spain, with a territory of only 181 sq. miles for a population of 55,000. Andorra offers a range of possibilities, from the oldest of age-old traditions to the most modern amenities for trade and shopping, from history and architecture to excursions into the mountains and forests, from gourmet food to skiing and other sports, and from crafts and folklore to the purest of ecological pastimes and holidays.

Andorra comes as a surprise at any time of the year, because of its ever-changing scenery. There is an incredible rage of hues and colours, in a well-balanced counterpoint between bustling streets and the calm, restful background of the mountain crests, all of it framed in a natural environment steeped in charm.

ANDORRA, ONE THOUSAND YEARS OF HISTORY

Legend has it that Andorra was founded by the Emperor, Charlemagne, in gratitude to the inhabitants of the valleys who had provided guides for his army in its fight against the Saracen. What is certain, is that the act of consecration of Seu d'Urgell Cathedral (in Spain), which dates from 839 A.D, lists the parishes in Andorra and indicates that they are part of the territory of the Counts of Urgell. From the 11th Century onwards, the Counts of Urgell gradually transferred their rights to the Church in Urgell, and they continued to do so until 1133 when Count Ermengol IV gave the Bishop of Urgell all his possessions in the Andorran valleys and asked the local people to pay homage to the Bishop and his successors as their lord and master. Because of certain war-

Le Pas de la Case.

ring tendencies among neighbouring lords vis-a-vis the Church in Urgell, the Bishop placed himself under the protection of the Caboet family and, in 1159, a treaty was signed by both parties, officially recognising the sovereignty of the Bishop of Urgell over Andorra and the gift of the Andorran valleys in fief to the House of Caboet. The heiress to the family's wealth, Arnalda de Caboet, married Viscount Annau de Castellbó and transferred to him the feudal rights over the valleys in Andorra. The daughter of this marriage, Ermessenda de Castelbó, married Count Roger Bernat de Foix and, in her turn, transferred to him the feudal rights over the Andorran valleys which she had inherited from her parents. After a succession of conflicts concerning sovereignty over Andorra, opposing the Count of Foix and the Bishop of Urgell, the *"Pareatge"* was signed on 8th September 1278, the first constitutional document in Andorra, defi-

ning the share of each of the lords of the territory in the economic, legal and military domains and requiring that the Andorran people pay the *"Qüèstia"* to each of the lords in alternate years. A decade later, another *"Pareatge"* was signed, clarifying some of the points in the previous document that had given rise to legal argument. The two documents provided a final solution to the disputes between the lords and all the conditions laid down by these acts are still in force today. Indeed, it is this document which ensures Andorra's institutional equilibrium.

In 1419, the men of Andorra requested from the Co-Princes the right to hold Council in order to resolve any problems arising in the community. As a result of the privilege granted by the Co-Princes, the *"Consell de la Terra"* was set up. This was the first parliamentary body in Andorra and, as time passed, was to become the

San Juan de Casellas, a superb example of Andorran Romanesque architecture.

"*Consell general*" consisting of representatives from each parish in the principality. In the 16th Century, the rights held by the Count of Foix passed to the Crown of France, when Henri II of Foix and Henri III of Navarre was proclaimed King Henri IV of France. His son, Louis XIII, confirmed the incorporation of the rights of the House of Caboet, Castelbó, Foix and Béarn into the rights of the Crown of France. Thus it was that the rights over Andorra, and its sovereignty, were shared, personally, between the Bishop of Urgell and the King of France who was the successor of the Counts of Foix. The structure was momentarily interrupted during the French Revolution but, on 27th March 1806 at the request of the Andorran people, Napoleon signed an imperial decree re-establishing the status of the co-principality.

On 22nd April 1866, the "New Reform" was promulgated, stipulating that the members of the *Consell general* would be elected by the "*caps de casa*" (heads of families) under a system of limited suffrage. On 17th July 1993, male universal suffrage was established for the election of members of the *Consell general*. Finally, under the terms of a decree signed by the co-princes on 14th April 1970, the women of Andorra were given the vote.

The traditional number of parishes (six) was increased to seven in 1978. They are **Canillo, Encamp, Ordino, La Massana, Andorra la Vella, San Julià de Lòria** and **Escaldes Engordany**. Each parish elects four *Consellers*

Generals and the twenty-eight general councillors make up the *Consell general* (or parliament) under the chairmanship of the *Síndic general* and *Sub-Síndic general*.

The co-princes, i.e. the heads of state of Andorra, delegate their functions to permanent represenatives resident in Seu d'Urgell and Perpignan respectively. They also appoint the *Viguiers* who live in the principality and are responsible for administering justice and ensuring public order.

Under the terms of a decree signed on 15th January 1981, the co-princes agreed to the setting up of a *Govern d'Andorra* (government) at the request of the Andorran people. The government is presided by the *Cap de Govern* and consists of four to six *Consellers de Govern* (ministers). The *Cap de Govern* is elected by the *Consell general*. In the same decree, it was specified that Andorra is a co-principality for which the two leaders are personally and equally responsible. The leaders are the **Bishop of Urgell** and the **Head of State of France** as successor to the Counts of Foix.

On 14th March 1993, three-quarters of the Andorran people decided, in a referendum, to consent to a draft constitution which would leave the two co-princes, the President of France and the Bishop of Seu de Urgell, nothing but a honorary role as representatives of the country. **Andorra is an independent, sovereign State** which can henceforth make its own political and economic decisions.

Near the Envalira Pass.

THE SPANISH PYRENEES

The Lanuza reservoir.

The Spanish side of the Pyrenees includes most of the highest peaks in the entire range e.g. **Pic d'Aneto** (11,076 ft.), **Las Tres Sorores** (10,904 ft.), **Posets** (10,956 ft.) etc. From West to East, the Spanish Pyrenees slope gently down through the Spanish **Basque Country**, **Navarre**, **Aragon** and **Catalonia**. On this side of the mountains, the scenery is more arid, and the undisputed kingdom of unspoilt nature, water, granite, limestone, and valleys.

Guipuzcoa is the most Pyrenean of the three Basque provinces. Ignoring geographical frontiers, the people enjoy the same culture on each side of the mountain. In Spain, though, the pride of the people and their independent character seem to be stronger. Incorporated into the Kingdom of Castile in the 14th Century, the Basque Country nevertheless retained a certain number of privileges in every field - administration, politics, religion and finance. The privileges confirmed the very special status of these provinces along the Atlantic seaboard but were taken away during the Civil War, and for thirty-nine years thereafter, in revenge for the uprisings fomented against General Franco. Nowadays, the Basque Country is one of the richest regions in Spain. It is also an autonomous region that boasts an equally fascinating past and present.

Beyond the border post at the St. James Bridge in **Hendaye** lies **Fuenterrabia**, the first of the fishing harbours inside Spain. **San Telmo's Castle**, the former residence of Emperor Charles V, is now a luxurious *parador*. The coastline is dotted with picturesque harbours such as **Pasajes, Orio, Guetaria** etc. One of them, **San Sebastian**, is now the main town in the Guipuzcoa region. Originally a naval base built to stand guard over the Franco-Spanish border, San Sebastian owed its expansion in the 19th Century to summer visits by the Kings of Spain. Its development as a seaside resort centred on the magnificent **La Concha** Beach.

Opposite: the Pic d'Aneto, the highest peak in the Pyrenean range with an altitude of 11,076 ft.

Scenery on the Spanish side of the Somport Pass.

The winter sports resort of Candanchu.

Opposite: Sallent, between Formigal and Lanuza (top).
Roncesvalles (bottom).

In the heart of the Atlantic side of the Pyrenees are the **mountain peaks of Anie** (8,138 ft.), **Orhy** (6,558 ft.), and **Mesa de los Tres Reyes** (7,910 ft), the highest in this part of the range. Beyond the **Col d'Ibaneta**, the road runs on to Santiago de Compostela, past countless Romanesque buildings. **Roncesvalles** (once a pilgrims' hostel), **Leyre** (the oldest monastery in Spain), and **Estella la Bella Sanguesa** are the finest examples of this architectural style. The capital of Navarre, **Pampluna**, is famous for the San Fermin Festival when the entire town seems to "let itself go". Its main buildings are a memorial to two thousand years of history and the Santa Maria Cathedral, town walls and fortress serve as reminders of an eventful past.

Nature, too, seems to provide her own form of architecture. Gouged into the limestone by a process of erosion, the **Three Arches in Lumbier** stand high above the Irati river gorge. Other natural beauty spots are cut into the landscape, among them **Foz de Nagore, Fos de Txintxurrunea, Arbayin,** and **Minchate**.

Upper Aragon is a land of mountain peaks above granite, schist or limestone slopes. Among the summits are **Aneto, Posets, Mulleres, Monte Perdido.** The lakes includes **Millares,** and **Creguena**. The ski resorts of **Candanchu, Formigal, Panticosa,** and **Valle del Astun** are very popular venues. Standing along in the South of the Bénasque Valley is the **Turbon Range** rising to an altitude of 8,099 ft. The **Ordesa National Park** covers an area of 2,200 hectares at the foot of the Los Tres Sorores range, in which the highest peak is Monte Perdido (altitude 10,904 ft). It is an animal reserve and a superb natural setting filled with waterfalls, gorges and a wide range of wild life, including large numbers of mountain goats.

The road to the pass at Le Somport is another of the roads leading to Santiago de Compostela in Galicia. Along the way is **Jaca** whose Romanesque cathedral gives the little town its heart and soul. A few miles away are the monasteries of **San Juan de la Peña** and **Santa Cruz de los Seros**, Romanesque buildings of particular interest.

In Catalonia, the Pyrenees are less sheer than in Aragon even though some of the peaks in the province of Gerone rise to altitudes of more than 9,425 ft. There are ski resorts near the Puigmal (alt. 9,454 ft.), in **Molina, Nuria, Valiter 2000**. The Benedictine monastery in **Ripoll** has a library that was once one of the richest in the whole of the Christian world. In Catalonia, the cathedrals are called "*Seo*". The ones in **Urgell**, **Lerida**, and **Gerone** are among the most outstanding. The **Aigues Tortes y Lago de San Maurico National Park** stretches over an area of 4 hectares. Dominated by the **Pic de Coma-Lo-Formo** (alt. 9,848 ft.), the countryside is full of contrasts, with impressive rock formations and tranquil lakes.

Just as admirable as the scenery and buildings is what might be called Pyrenean Spanish cuisine, to which we must pay homage. Despite the fact that each province has its own specialities, the dishes have one feature in common - their Spanish flavour. Let us just mention the pork meat products, Navarre-style trout, Basque-style meat dishes, game, ham, *menestra* (a sort of stew), cod *a la Canigou* etc. Any list of sweets must include *turron* (nougat), curdled milk, and Pyrenean forest fruits (redcurrants, strawberries, blackberries and raspberries). And last but not least there is Roncal cheese from Navarre.

Near the Col du Pourtalet lies the village of Lanuza
which was deserted when it was partially flooded by the rise in the water level during the building of the dam.

Mountain peaks around the corrie at Gavarnie (Hautes-Pyrénées).

Now that we have come to the end of this journey through the Pyrenees,
it is easier to understand why the mountains, with their wealth of natural
habitats and scenery, are a constant source of enjoyment and delight for local
people and visitors alike. From the Atlantic seaboard to the Mediterranean
coast, you only have to let yourself be carried along by the beauty of the peaks
and the ever-changing landscapes to understand just why we have described
them as the "Wonderful Pyrenees".

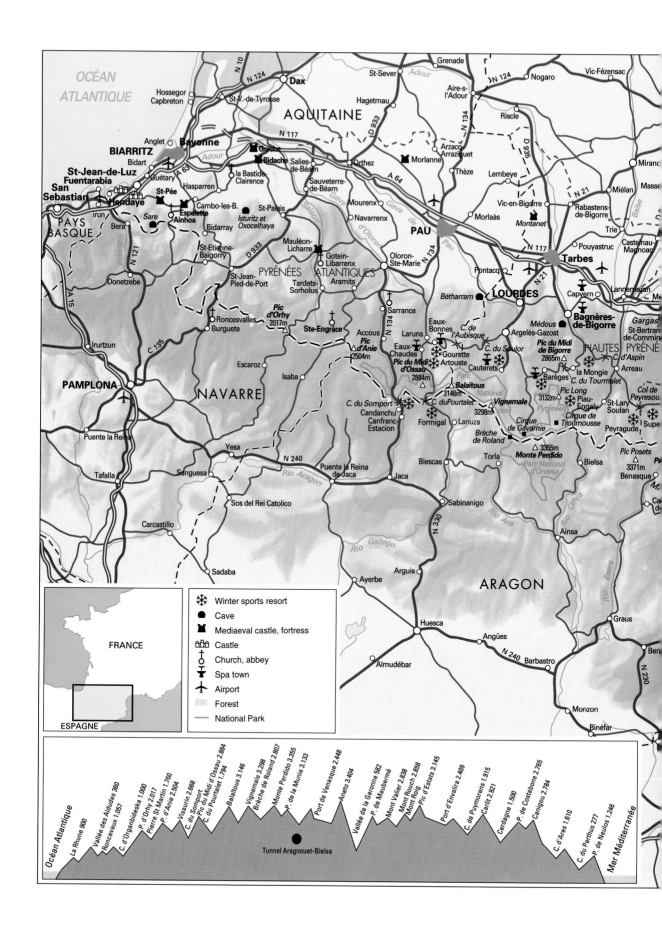

OCÉAN ATLANTIQUE

AQUITAINE

PAYS BASQUE

PYRÉNÉES ATLANTIQUES

NAVARRE

ARAGON

HAUTES PYRÉNÉES

FRANCE

ESPAGNE

Winter sports resort
Cave
Mediaeval castle, fortress
Castle
Church, abbey
Spa town
Airport
Forest
National Park

Grenade
St-Sever
Dax
Nogaro
Vic-Fézensac
Aire-s-l'Adour
Riscle
Hagetmau
Arzacq-Arraziguet
Thèze
Morlanne
Lembeye
Mirand
Masse
Vic-en-Bigorre
Miélan
Rabastens-de-Bigorre
Trie
Castelnau-Magnoac
Pouyastruc
Tarbes
Lannemezan
M
Capvern
Bagnères-de-Bigorre
Gargas
St-Bertran-de-Commin
Col de Peyresou
Arreau
C. d'Aspin
la Mongie
C. du Tourmalet
Barèges
St-Lary-Soulan
Supe
Peyragude
Pic Posets
3371m
P
Benasque
M
Ca
de
Bielsa
Ainsa
Graus
Ber
Bena
Monzon
Binéfar

Hossegor
Capbreton
St-V.-de-Tyrosse
Guiche
Bidache
Salies-de-Béarn
Orthez
Morlanne
Pau
Montanet
BIARRITZ
Bidart
Guétary
Anglet
Bayonne
la Bastide-Clairence
Sauveterre-de-Béarn
Mourenx
Navarrenx
PAU
Morlaàs
St-Jean-de-Luz
Fuentarabia
San Sebastian
Hendaye
irun
St-Pée
Espelette
Ainhoa
Sare
Cambo-les-B.
St-Palais
Isturitz et Oxocelhaya
Hasparren
Bidarray
Bera
Mauléon-Licharre
Gotein-Libarrenx
Oloron-Ste-Marie
Pontacq
Béarn
St-Etienne-Baïgorry
PYRÉNÉES
Tardets-Sorholus
Aramits
Bétharram
LOURDES
Donetzebe
St-Jean-Pied-de-Port
Sarrance
Médous
Argelès-Gazost
Pic du Midi de Bigorre
2865m
Irurtzun
Roncesvalles
Burguete
Pic d'Orhy
2017m
Ste-Engrâce
Accous
Pic d'Anie
2504m
Eaux-Bonnes
C. de l'Aubisque
Laruns
C. du Soulor
Gourette
Artouste
Cauterets
Pic Long
Piau-Engaly
3132m
Escaroz
Isaba
Eaux-Chaudes
Pic du Midi d'Ossau
2884m
Balaïtous
3146m
C. du Somport
C. du Pourtalet
Vignemale
3298m
Cirque de Troumousse
PAMPLONA
NAVARRE
C. du Somport
Candanchu
Canfranc-Estacion
Formigal
Lanuza
3298m
Brèche de Roland
Cirque de Gavarnie
3355m
Monte Perdido
Pic Posets
Puente la Reina
Yesa
Rio Aragon
N 240
Puente la Reina de Jaca
Jaca
Biescas
Torla
Parc National d'Ordesa
Bielsa
Tafalla
Sanguesa
Sabinanigo
Benasque
Sos del Rei Catolico
Rio Gallego
Rio Ara
Rio Cinca
Ainsa
Rio Esera
Carcastillo
Arguis
ARAGON
Sadaba
Ayerbe
Huesca
Angües
Graus
Almudébar
N 240
Barbastro
Monzon
Binéfar

Océan Atlantique
La Rhune 900
Vallée des Aldudes 360
Roncevaux 1.057
C. d'Organbideska 1.000
P. d'Orhy 2.017
Pierre St-Martin 1.760
P. d'Anie 2.504
Visaurin 2.668
C. du Somport
Pic du Midi d'Ossau 2.884
C. du Pourtalet 1.794
Balaïtous 3.146
Vignemale 3.298
Brèche de Roland 2.807
Monte Perdido 3.355
P. de la Munia 3.133
Port de Venasque 2.448
Aneto 3.404
Vallée de la Garonne 582
P. de Maubermé
Mont Valier 2.838
Mont Rouch 2.858
Mont Roig
Pic d'Estats 3.145
Port d'Envalira 2.409
C. de Puymorens 1.915
Carlit 2.921
Cerdagne 1.500
P. de Costabona 2.785
Canigou 2.784
C. d'Ares 1.610
C. du Perthus 277
P. de Neulos 1.246
Mer Méditerranée
Tunnel Aragnouet-Bielsa

MIDI - PYRÉNÉES

HAUTE - GARONNE

ARIÈGE

LANGUEDOC - ROUSSILLON

AUDE

PYRÉNÉES ORIENTALES

CATALOGNE

Parc National
d'Aigues Tortes

MER MÉDITERRANÉE

Grenade
Montastruc
Graulhet
Réalmont
Lacaune
Bédarieux
l'Isle-Jourdain
N 124
Lavaur
St-Paul-Cap-de-Joux
Brassac
la Salvetat-s-A.
TOULOUSE
N 126
Castres
St-Pons-de-Thomières
Béziers
Muret
Revel
Mazamet
N 112
Puisserguier
Rieumes
Montgiscard
Villefranche-de-Lauragais
N 113
Saissac
CARCASSONNE
Narbonne
Auterive
Castelnaudary
A 61
Lézignan-Corbières
Carbonne
N 20
Saverdun
Montréal
N 117
Aurignac
D 119
D 118
Narbonne-Plage
Salies-du-Salat
le Mas-d'Azil
Pamiers
Mirepoix
Limoux
Durban-Corbières
Gruissan
dens
D 117
la Bastide-de-Sérou
St-Jean-des-Verges
D 613
Monthoumet
Port-la-Nouvelle
St-Girons
D 117
Foix
Roquefixade
Couiza
Rennes-les-Bains
Tuchan
Port-Leucate
Montgaillard
Puivert
Rennes-le-Château
Peyrepertuse
A 9
Port-Barcarès
Castillon-en-Couserans
Bédeilhac
Lavelanet
Quillan
Quéribus
Salses
Massat
Montségur
D 117
St-Paul-de-Fenouillet
Tarascon
Ussat-les-Bains
Axat
Niaux
Lombrives
PERPIGNAN
Aulus-les-Bains
Lordat
Aguzou
Millas
Canet-Plage
Miglos
Ax-les-Thermes
Usson
Salardu
N 20
Pic d'Estats
3145m
Fontrabiouse
N 116
Vinça
Serrabone
Esterri d'Aneu
Prades
Pic Carlit
les Angles
Olette
St-Michel-de-Cuxa
Soldeu
Pyrénées 2000
Vernet-les-Bains
Collioure
Port-Vendres
Andorra-la-Vella
C.de 2921m
Puymorens
les Canalettes
St-Martin-du-Canigou
le Boulou
Banyuls
Pas de la Caze
Font-Romeu
Pic du Canigou
2784m
Céret
Cerbère
N 2
Mont-Louis
Amélie-les-Bains
Portbou
Puigcerda
Saillagouse
D 115
la Jonquera
Sort
Bourg-Madame
Prats-de-Mollo
N 260
Martinet
Cadaqués
la Seu d'Urgell
la Molina
N 260
Ribes de Freser
Col d'Arès
Roses
remp
Sant Pau de Segurie
Figueras
l'Escala
Berga
Ripoll
Olot
Banyoles
Bassella
Rio Ter
Artesa de Segre
Ponts
N 152
Girona
Palafrugel
Cervera
Vich
Anglès
Tarrega
N 11
Platja d'Aro
Igualada
Manresa
S. Feliu de Guixols
Terrassay
Sabadell
A 7
N 11
Mataro
0   50 Km
Badalona
BARCELONA
© IKEN cartographie

TABLE OF CONTENTS

Also by **Jean-Pierre Bouchard** (author and/or photographer)

Périgord, terre de mémoire (Ed. Fanlac, Périgueux) (English translation available)
Photographs taken as part of the International Film Festival in Cannes and distributed by Gamma.
Périgord noir (with Roland Giraud and Jean Carmet) (Ed. Ouest-France)
Hollywood en Périgord (No. 1 of the *Journal du Périgord*)
Le bassin d'Arcachon (Ed. Ouest-France) (German translation available)
Les bastides du Périgord (Ed. Ouest-France)
La route des vins de Bordeaux (Ed. Ouest-France) (English title - "Claret Country". German translation also available)
Saint-Emilion (Ed. Ouest-France) (Translated into English and German)
Biarritz (Ed. Ouest-France)
Pau (Ed. Ouest-France)
Aimer la Préhistoire en Périgord (Ed. Ouest-France) (Translated into English and German)
Aimer le Quercy (Ed. Ouest-France) (Translated into English and German)
Le Quercy (Ed. Ouest-France)
Aimer Sarlat (Ed. Ouest-France) (Translated into English and German)
Aimer Les Eyzies, capitale mondiale de la Préhistoire (Ed. Ouest-France) (German and English translations available)
Aimer la Gironde, Bordeaux et sa région (Ed. Ouest-France) (Translated into English and German)
La Gironde (Ed. Ouest-France)
La grande cuisine du Bordelais (Ed. Solar)
Aimer le pays cathare (Ed. Ouest-France) (Translated into English, German and Spanish)
Le Pays cathare (Ed. Ouest-France)
Les Cathares (Ed. Ouest-France) (Translated into English and German)
Aimer les Pyrénées (Ed. Ouest-France) (Translated into English, German and Spanish)
Les Pyrénées (Ed. Ouest-France)
Aimer l'Aveyron (Ed. Ouest-France)
Participated in the international exhibition entitled "The Birth of Art in Europe" organised by the *Union latine*.
Specialist publications on psychology, psychiatry, criminology and sexology.

Drawings are by **Rudy Presa**.

Cet ouvrage a été achevé d'imprimer par l'Imprimerie Pollina à Luçon (85) - n° 64580 - B
I.S.B.N. 2.7373.1400.3 - Dépôt légal : mars 1994
N° d'éditeur : 2789.01.03.03.94